RAISE
RACE
RAYS
RAZE

Essays Since 1965

Random House New York

Essays Since 1965
Imamu Amiri Baraka
(LeRoi Jones)

ISBN: 0-394-46222-X
Library of Congress Catalog Card Number: 70-140714

Some of these essays first appeared in *Onyx, Black World, Black Scholar, Journal of Black Poetry, Black Newark,* and *Black Power Revolt.* "Negro Theater Pimps Get Big Off Nationalism" was published by Third World Press. "Nationalism Vs PimpArt" first appeared in *The New York Times.* Copyright © 1969 by the New York Times Company. "Technology & Ethos" first appeared in *Amistad 2,* published by Random House, Inc.

Manufactured in the United States of America

35798642

First Edition

Sifa Ina Ote Mtu Weusi
Sifa Ina Ote Maulana
Sifa Ina Ote Kawaida

Contents

RAISE
RACE
RAYS
RAZE

Essays Since 1965

Newark Courthouse—'66 Wreck (Nigger Rec Room)

Newark CourtHouse Mornings, when you get down past Broad Street to Italian City Hall you see the basic conflict of America. Early morning appearance makes the niggers shuffling sleepily toward their other place in America (What Other?), the ct. house-jailhouse syndrome.

Our people look tired, bewildered and grey rusty in this kind of morning, shuffling into the slaughter house. The buildings whities house their "justice" in are Greek, or fake Greek. Their laws, their sense of "self" is still from there. Greek. The first "sophisticated" liars. The "new" flowering of White Nationalism.

9:45 Judge Jew is still not in. The few cops in the
mostly empty court sit smoking. The youngest, the black
haired ginnie-stereotype (too punkish to be Mafioso . . .
hence a shambler after pure-dee light) . . . smokes a
long black prestige cigar. His fingers swagger. The rest
are older, washed out, deadbeat court cops happy to be
sitting and lolling.

Redfaced Oirishmens & swarthy Italians make up the
bulk of the force. Those bitter niggers make their living
that way, not yet on the scene. Neither is Judge Narol.

On these mornings you see our people in their famous
casual agonies. This is a municipal Ct., Part 2. For hand-
ling light work, creating (a disturbance . . . ie just *say*
you are a man) can get you time. Maybe 3 mos. if Judge
Narol don't like your looks. That's irony I guess. Time for
Creating. Also they walk you off for bashing each other,
or thinking about bashing them. (I told a friend—don't
even raise your voice, unless you're going to kill them—
the process is against us, as form. This is true.)

But Time is the one thing given at these lower cts., only
time. That is the form. You are stupid ignorant or senti-
mental to even consider pausing your mind near some
idea of *justice*. This is their justice. This is their right.
To kill us, if we miss a step, if we balk, at the use we have
served these last three centuries.

In these cts. there are not too many crimes. Most of the
charges are, in fact, lies, or blown out of human proportion, to specify the term of the black man's oppression.

I had come down, this second time in 1966, with two
friends arrested the night before for CREATING (a disturbance. WHAT? kind of disturbance?) Asking policemen why they stopped these friends of mine in my car.
That *WHY?* at any level can cost you time. The Irish-Italo
street riders cannot abide a black man asking this question. The answer is too complicated. That is, its simplicity
would hide too much.

. . . The flag is crooked. The yng wopcop has his foot
propped up on the witness box. His Honor has not yet
arrived. 10:00. More black people drift in.
The WHY is some kind of assault-aggression to these po-
licemens. They can not take even that. Nor will they look
you in the eye. Nor will they *ever* come at you one on one.
Even they are not that simpleminded. They are coarse
women w/dicks at their sides, tied on their hips.

Two weeks ago I watched the same Narol give out time
to Black People. For anything ("just get them off the
streets"). The least display of manhood, nay even just self
conviction, was enough to aggravate the poppers & Narol
gave a big husband 10 days for thinking the proceedings
were over before they were. "What're you a wise guy?" The
level, the address, to the world, the tone of absolute disease
lingering heavily in these rooms strikes you dumb at first.
But that's one point. You cannot protest humanly, rationally, or even intellectually.
You walk before (I mean this) debased lower animals
who think themselves (you guessed it) GODS. They will
strike you down. They will shout at you, their command
of human relationships is so shaky, they will (on dimly
lit Washington streets) jump away in terror at an African
Elder's cane, even though they are Six Feet Six, w/brother
hairy bigteeth on a leash, and have a gun, blackjack, and
another similar looking chump-partner waiting for them
in car down the street. Yes. So insecure, and sure of their
guilt.
Jewish lawyers come in. (Still connected to us by that
desert experience; they follow niggers with wet sucking
nozzles stuck in the niggers' throats. The jews love us so.)
Two lovely Black girls.
10:29 The Judge Has Arrived!!!
First "Mushy Callahan" brought a "bum" for *Creating*,

who turned out to be merely a Negro waiting for a bus. ("Take yr hands out yr pocket," this was the cigar fondler getting his note.) The nigger says, "I was just waiting for the bus, and this guy comes up and starts talking rough to me, so I talked rough to him. Bum? Man, I was just comin' home from work. I work in a paintbrush factory, it's not a good idea to wear your good clothes."

Mushy sez, "Well, yr honor, he looked suspicious."

The disturbance?

The Nigger's personality was making noise in the night air. It disturbed Mushy. His red nose twirled with weather data, and oppression formulae.

"O.K. case dismissed . . . but watch who yr talking to mister."

"Yeh."

That lightened the air, and niggers buzzed warily. But nobody got optimistic. Next was Leroy Parker, for similar charges, who got 15 days for being black, poor and raggidy. Fifteen days, and Roy just stood with his lip poked out hearing some more shit, like he heard all his life. Fifteen days for being black and poor and raggidy. That is why we are all penalized; and the last two categories are completely arbitrary, that is, they depend on the context, the little political social organization of our lives, which is dependent on who we are. Who would construct a system(?) which made people poor and raggidy, which kept people sick and perverted and unable to taste of the sweet rise of life, as it evolves, and carries the ripe spirits with it to new light? But more important, to us Black People, who would accept such as "their lot," who would accept, and *be* what such a system demanded? What people would *allow* themselves to be so debased? *We make what we are.*

John McKinney, Drunk in the PRR.

"Stay sober, John. 15 Days."

Wilbur Sweetwine, Drunk in the PRR.

> "What's the matter
> with you, Wilbur? You
> drink liquor."

> Which be The Jew

is his paternal loving-ness. 15 Days. The cold white prose-
cutor in concrete evil.

Why are these things so? Black People, why are we the
victims? Ask your selves.

James Harrison, 37 year old black man. Drunk on Mul-
berry Street. Why? The prosecution runs his biography.
No Record. In Newark 3 years. Two Young Children.
"Job." 30 days suspended, to attend A. A. meetings until
further notice.

Ed Hawthorne, 50 year old black man. Driving while
under the influence of (?) $230. Fine, revoke license two
years.

Diane Parker, 23 year old black girl, No charge, 100$.
appearance next Wed. complaintant wasn't there.

Wait a minute. Who are these judges? Who should
order your life but your selves. The better, best, part of
your feelings about the world. The persecutor and the per-
secuted can only have the same judge under threat of
death. To be before *this* judge we must have already been
judged: And found guilty! *Guilty!*

Now a loud call: "Schenley versus Schenley." This is
husband vs wife. The Black Man versus The Black
Woman. A public show of our estrangement and debase-
ment. The loss of our black family.

Who are the men of this world? This black sister brings
her troubles to the white man. To hoteljockeys like Aaron
Narol, shantung judge of the subject peoples, a little be-
mused, tolerant like you would be of a blackhead, which
is how he deals. The relentless boring sameness of his

petty mind. The slow screech of the wheels in his trape-
zoidal noggin.

The story is told. About separation and welfare. The
judge suppresses a laugh. (He is judging, just a minute.)
Nine white men stand around the bench listening: lawyers, cops, clerks, official ctroom drifters.

"He hit her in the breast with a chair, yr honor."

"She tried to stick me."

"One year probation . . . suspended sentence . . .
$30.00 dollars a week." He says, supressing a laugh.

Here is a 33 year old nigger boy named Julius who has
violated his parole. "Six months Essex cty penitentiary."
It happened so quick. Julius was led in and out. His life
altered, or arranged to be the same. Narol not quite even
looking up. These are the stalls. The anonymous banal
boring horror of slavery. The dispatch, no this way, hurry
up goddamyou, pushing he stumbles into the wall, shaking in front of the stand, to hear the six months. The sailing smells like wine. What is it Julius had done . . . I
mean, in the first place? They walk him out back to jail.
He's gone.

A 60 year old man stands there now in a janitor suit.
His head is definitely bent. Narol says, "You gonna be a
good boy?" Amused, as are the others, all the others. Even
the niggers whose father this is, and whose lives are
tainted with similar despair. They, also, smile. More Time.

A little light stuff: Willie vs Officer Yablonsky. Resist-
ing. Yeh? Hmm. "I told him to get out of his car, yrhonor.
He sez why. He went past the light." Yeh? Hmmm. 100-
dollar fine. Yr lucky, fella.

In the short time of two weeks I had occasion to go
back to the Municipal court three more times. Once because two friends of mine were arrested when they were
driving to the delicatessen to get fruit juice and sand-
wiches to tighten them up during a long night of prop
making. An officer named Capone and one of the short
red sons of Erin stopped the car, made them pull over,

get out, and identify themselves, because (these cops said later) these fellahs "looked peculiar."

Even after it was proven that the car (price $56.00) they were driving was not stolen, but belonged to an Everett Jones who they knew and who lived in the same house they did, the "rollers," embarrassed and angry because they had picked up a couple of niggers (whose friends soon showed up on the spot) who not only were more intelligent and articulate than they, but who also despised them quite matter of factly, trumped up some charge in front of the car, the name of which they wd tell no one, and then dragged the two friends off in their car, saying that no one had better try to follow them where they were going.

Luckily everybody did know exactly where they were going: the precinct on Washington St. When we got there Capone and the Police Lt. were hunched over the front desk figuring out what the two niggers could be charged with. They went over a small list of suitable offenses, the lieutenant giving Capone the pros and cons, the mitigatings, circling around each offense. During this period we tried to find out what the two men were charged with, the lieutenant, supposedly the wise man of the joint, turned caveman red and started screaming as how he wd arrest everybody or everyblackbody in the place.

I notice one thing in talking to policemen. When they are angry, talk to them very quietly, very very quietly, calmly (even if you're getting ready to kill them) it makes them even angrier, it drives them past their "reason," that you are trying to be reasonable, when faced with himself the beast.

Work Notes—'66

The total climate of america repulses collective efforts by black men. The ego struggles & work dispersal due to a need to work for white men to earn a living are the biggest defeaters. Ego struggles meaning black men cannot yet choose actual leaders among themselves. Leaders who are right to do things, who have the nature of movement, and the need the daring the destiny to make things work. All with any information claim the right to be leaders. And this is defeatist.

White science works to keep this so. We look at each other with the suspicion of white shadows in our faces. Why did you say this? We ask as if a white thing prompted each of us to say and do. We cannot rely on each other, and read newspapers look at white people even disgusted, for answers anyway.

We must submit to ourselves. and understand the beauty of our own necessity. It is there. We must submit to each other, and let one of us, as specialists in particular fields, go on out with the rest following. We must see that work gets done. Now. We will die with (or at the hands of) white people, otherwise.

. . .

Leadership classes. From all "Classes."
Books by committee (Ishmael Reed's concept). Students must select books. Each must contribute a chapter, from actual research and life inspiration. We need all kinds of books. We need all kinds of black intelligence complexes. History, Creative Motif, Socio-Political Thrusts, must be studied, detailed, and set down in quick books, to be distributed by us, as cheaply as possible.

Specific gaps must be filled in. Communications, for instance. How to get to black people, despite the killing competition of television-radio. Radio is "black," so it is less of a washer at this point. Although, for sure, the wash comes through on all levels of Western communications media.

For even though Radio is "black," to the extent that we hear our own sounds, &c., still make no mistake the boy is most always in control and shooting his stuff through. Both "invisibly," ie commercials, news, disk jockeys' light editorials during their music-soul spiel. Even so there are out an out Shots like Dr. Robert Scalopino WWRL action, with the hot white word, re anything.

Television is purer white, the black shots fully oriented, and less than 1% of any warm blackness coming through. You might see Smokey or James Brown a couple times. But mostly there is a steady deadly whiteness beaming forth.

For this reason our written words strive for the speed of the electronics media. The picture book and comic book are to be worked on now to get in our own black registrations. The performance of poets &c. is best *live* to the black audience (as we create one). Better to publish mimeographs left around free on doorsteps and for five cents than depend on the Western book form, which finds only "intellectuals," and worse.

Films, Records, Picture books, we have to work on, and get them into the communities. For this reason stores, communications centers are worth a great deal to us. A black newsstand must be a fixture in all of our communities, either through a ready agent for blackness (colored owned), or the revolutionaries must come to own them somehow.

The Educational/School (University) concept at one end. The performance, lecture, reading concept at the other. We are in need of the organization of black consciousness, wherever, and in whatever guise. Teaching and Delighting. But the goal must always be movement . . . into . . . To get in, to move, and move our own, energies and people.

Go into the communities. Attract through the clarity of your vision, and, of course, through the rightness of your actions. Groups must set up as families or as friends. Formality must be dispensed with except as the form of encounter dictates. How (to) you attract the people? What can you do with them then?

The Block Association concept works as long as you have an energizing element (part of revolutionary group, instructor, &c. women work well in this) to stay right in the middle of the organization . . . suggesting, initiating, actually doing the brunt of the work, since in the general black communities apathy and sensual compensation are the functional lifestyle.

CREATING

> To agitate. Attend political, antipoverty social projection civil rights &c &c *meetings*. Distribute black images.
>
> *Always* attack (whether publicly

or anonymously even if
conciliation and "brother
hood" w/certain Toms
serves a public end.
Extend present situations. In-
troduce revolutionary insight
into "problems." Make things
black and white. Simplify and
clarify. Again, make a hu-
manist point if needed, but
keep revolutionary goals (and
attack active) always in sight.

Provide Black Alternatives: to any white actions, facts, or circumstance.
Whether through word or
deed. Work with facts. Bring
the facts to bear on environment, and situations prob-
lematic and useful to black
people and black revolutionaries.

Art must serve to illuminate and educate

Enlighten by delightin
Stimulate: the image must carry and
carry us to the goal the place
desired. Each aspect of black
life must have light shed on
it, must be analyzed must
make the pain of recognizing
the exact place of our cruci-
fixion, the exact sloth and
cowardliness, the precise ugliness and ignorance. But
also, let the black beauty glow
through, whether attained or
desired what we are and what

we all *can* be. Stress evolution, what the world can be
in strong and beautiful hands.

Posters.   Anywhere, and especially in a definite place,
recognized by people as a place where wisdom,
&c. is got.

Plays.   Anywhere. But also as responses to shit white
people run. Plays for board of education, for
police station, for draft board, for junky mus-
ters, always provide alternatives. And with them,
or as them, the post white, or post american
form.

All performances readings, &c. shd always be set off with
music dancing. Black music dancing, general open head-
edness to set the right black tone. Open the face to what
you must put into it. Put the situation itself in relief.

Poetry and Karma

The poetry of the world reflects the people(s) of the world. Their spirit and their lives, and in their various postures, and in *whatever* form, wherever there is human life.

American poetry reflects American lives. The various kinds, as they are found, in America, from whatever voices. Each voice is a place, in America, in the totality of its image. All these voices are different facets of that image. Tho the whole, it should be clear, is like that of the final Dorian Gray, stretched out on the floor in his Victorian vine, drowned in his own putresence and evil. The portrait changes, miraculously back to the fair, the uplifted. Dorian himself is the reality.

So in America some of the voices which seek to describe it are like Dorian himself, since they are real, and reflect the reality of place, in a variety of forms and through a variety of methods, and then there are other voices, who like the static unrealistic image of evil Dorian reflect in unreality some kind of stunted "prettiness" for the monsterman. His dead congealing eyes are seen to dance in bright blue song, so twitter some lacey vultures for whom rotted flesh is green dripping ecstasy. Pretty patterns of weak vomit, fashioned into brief emotionless places in a universe we must finally understand is beautiful, and understandable, and perfectible through wisdom and knowledge.

Merica is to die, soon. All good men want it to fall. The very continent will sink one day. This western sub-branch in its "rise" to material comfort has abandoned its Gods. Its religious poetry is trite and stupid: embarrassing. They have no need for God. Nor do this sub-branch, these last people of a spent cycle, understand any more what Art is, since they have cast it out of their lives. So that their poets who would come near where beauty truly lies must also cast them down and masquerade as captive niggers.

The poetry in America is America's heart. Americans die from heart failure. No hearts, abruptly. (Quiet as it's kept they never had any to begin with.) A centuries old defect.

The poetry of straightup Christian White America is White Christian Poetry. A poetry that runs its madness elopement in search of the sweetness of dead/ness. The chitterwhimper of some kind of highly domesticated animals who laugh or growl when near human beings. Tiny hairless flesheaters who eat their doo-doo with little fingers extended. They are so cool.

They have a theory of life that revolves around their missing dicks. The statues watch them and smile. They smile at the statues, the cunning little fountains in their white overseas ghettos, where balding superfeelers "from the states" the gentle conquerors, malinger in studied preciousness. The little dingling rhythms of their lives a horrible static between the glorious stations of human development to a more sensitive form of life.

Their traditions, from The West, and their lack of fire music. Staid studies "academic" rhythms, passed across desks like canceled stamps. You listen to corny music lessons in Carnegie Hall. No life has existed in that music for centuries. Perhaps never. This music celebrates no God. The music of the poems celebrates no God. But Devils.

Do you know what Greek Music sounded like?
English Music.
Italians and Germans made their music.
Spanish music is hotter, from the Moors.
There is blood in the drum.

As opposed to the "romantic" dribble of Wagner, the inchoate cave yells of a cold people idealizing horror . . . the baring of superhairy ches'es, &c. Poetry is music grown a little less abstract, or less "free" perhaps. Words can be "tagged," after a time, as simple instruction. Tho the "melodies" of Western Music are so tagged by their inventors' intention which is to have *everything known*. Music thinker Ernest Borneman said once about Black Music that it was "the withholding of all signposts," ie, we are natural men who we know can never go the same way, and certainly not again. Tell me all the things in the world? Or better, tell me all the feelings that exist? What feelings do not exist? A catalogue of life is an endless sound, which could be broken up into nothing. No-things.

So Poetry in America, like music in America, must go from any point toward one "thing" to its reconnector (opposite) at the other end of the scale. Fire and Ice. There is a poetry of Fire and Ice. There is a music of these, and their variations and reappearances. The Poetry Of The Dead and The Poetry Of The Living.

America is a place of dead and living beings. The dead and dying beings create a magnetism for death and sickness in America. The Living, growing beings create a magnetism for beauty love work thought: Life. We wear the Life Sign, the ankh.

Living Rhythms Dying Rhythms.

The way we live our lives taps out our personal life rhythm. Literally, our hearts, keep the beat of living, carry its rhythm. It's even why you pat your foot. When I say "The way we live our lives," I mean The Way, but also, in what manner, a simple how? As specific as a Social Worker's questionnaire, that *how* can be answered, and seen, and understood.

People object to other people's poems because they do not like the way those people live, or because they do not understand: similar biases. The Beatnik versus The American, though they are both right. (This is white poetry I'm speaking of now.) Richard Wilbur and Allen Ginsberg could hang out in a number of joints, in common, and laugh about it, being "accomplished poets" at home as meaning-horns for the inch of filth they represent. I do not mean this derogatorily, I mean that they are A Club, and separate from their Lords, but that they have tales (tails) which are similar. And tied end to end a string of rats, all the way down the line. Their music from the different corners of the room. They are a race, of a sub-branch, really, and all of them, and all of the tradition they can remember, is merely tail hairs from a long gone horse.

At the beginning of the century the modern poets were trying to break into the rhythms of this century. The schools teach that the break through is just being made. In the white academies most of the modern poets that are canonized are not as modern as white poets like Eliot and Pound and Williams. Their legitimate successors and improvers are still thought about as "way out." We are just passing through the era of McKinley in most college poet-classes.

The poets who have the most Power in America are post McKinley age poets, but just barely. They reflect the reality of unreality. They are the paperflowers that decorate monster vomit. They prate about dead references to dead reality. They still have not recognized that they are only Clark Kent; or rather they still think Clark is cool even without his contemporary fantasy change. The *real* Superman committed suicide.

There are Peace Corps poets, SNCC poets, Housing Project Poets, Poets that reflect the deathly stillness of brainfever, or the floating plastic pussycities above Yonkers where the "cream" of White Feeling lives, in its self-hypnotized sterility.

Chinese Poetry and Anglo Saxon Poetry were Avant Garde in 1915, The Destruction Of Localism. The Missouri lad who wishes himself into a Saville Row funeral, or the Idaho boy who left his Barbarian people, ditto the Missourian, in search of CULTURE, knowing there was none where they had come from. And so replenished their streams. Or Williams who understood that mere concentration on the Local, presumed it to be General, and again generally descriptive of the world. He wanted attention. Which should be natural, to look around when you find yourself somewhere.

But listen to their music. (You are going to play Mahler? I don't have the time . . . or Webern, that tiny eye, hand, for everything, and so much drops off. Those dits and das, Morse again. To tell us what??? that all of it is not coming in. Like Zukofsky, his little coughs and smidges of reality, with the whole of the planet shaking around his ears, his people about to be destroyed, and we get the tiny dihs and dahs, the static creepy anemic beeps.

But here we have been talking about intelligence already, and neglecting the dumb stone of traditional white materialism. I mean the intelligence of loss, "sensing the loss," observing it, no matter the cover story, which they will explain as "human," ie the justification for all this bullshit.

They can no longer "cover" the world. Like Webern's occasional sparklers in a night of alien recognition, it is well known now that The West is bare thin streaks of meaning, except as it proposes an opposite for itself, which is already growing and somewhat understood.

The Cult Of Themselves has died out, except in its continuation through any mode of their expression, even in more subtle, or the subtlest of ways. I mean their thing is always pushed, but now, and for some time, it has been put in the context of despair; Samuel Beckett is a precise white poet, or Robert Creeley, William Burroughs or Ed Sanders, or Allen Ginsberg, or Herman Melville. They tell it mostly like it is. Empty furies; Spent Husks, unbelievable evil, the love of SELF (destruction). They describe a race, better than anyone else. They describe themselves: Kafka, Joyce, Proust, Mann. They continue. Nathanael West, John Rechy, Hubert Selby, Jack Kerouac. They continue, and show you, this is latest, what they think, and what and who they are. You wanted to know?? Well they tell you always, in whatever they do. You think a soup can is not art? Well, what about it? What does that mean? It is Art? It is the identification that is finally important. What kind of Art. What must it be and what must they think it is and represents for it to be Art, and what must they be to be there, digging and as a result of such digging, what homes, &c. hobbies do they have??

Art is a highvoltage culture-reflect. Poetry the mode of thought trying to spiritualize itself. Sound-rhythm (image) in imitation of the *elementals* of the universe. So it digs deeper, goes to, beyond, the edge of "meaning" recreates language feeling, to bring us closer to these elementals, beyond where the "intellect" reaches.

White poetry is intellectual and physical for the most part. In imitation of its creator's genius. Physical in its attempt to make F O R M S which endure past their meanings as organic creations. The intellect can only deal finally with the physicality of the universe; the brain is a thing.

White poetry is a poetry of ratiocination, or post-voli-

tional ratiocination (get to that). The intellectual is sorely
limited. It does not get to the wellsprings of knowledge
(it is a corny "activity" actually). It fits slower beings,
but the swiftest and surest knowledge is what Hegel
thought of as intuition. The intimacies of spirit. (For instance, the worst parts of this essay are caused by me
"thinking" . . . like this part.) Do without do-ing.

White poetry is like white music (for the most part,
and even taking into account those "imitations" I said,
which are all as valid as W C Williams writing about Bunk
Johnson's band. Hear the axles turn, the rust churned and
repositioned. The death more subtly or more openly
longed for. Creeley's black box, Olson's revivification of
the dead, Ginsberg's screams at his own shadowy races
or the creepier elements completely covered up with silver
rubied garbage artifacts and paintings and manners and
ideas, my god, they got a buncha ideas, and really horrible crap between them and anything meaningful. They
probably belch without feeling.

Americans long for feeling, tho they cannot have it, being anti-spiritual, nor do they know that they do long.
Except their white poets, the best of them, also, want to
feel, more conspicuously.

Black People in the West are also subjected to the mind
sores, their overflow as art or actual pop art of the western repertory theater, which be but a nasty lil' agent in
your house . . . the devil's own voice and image, piped
constantly into your home. (Whether the "Educational"
or the commercial, they are all *training devices*, like they
say, visual aids.)

And all part of what they think of as (some kind of)
beauty. You get their "beauty," at all levels . . . which is
garbage, poison, and nonsense. In order to make the black
poetry, the poetry of spirit and feeling, it is absolutely
necessary to sidestep white stuff and open up into a purer
more natural world. (Do you understand that they teach

you their neuroses and madness??? I mean do you understand, that that is being done, with each second and that
our black children suck it in, running around the streets
in batman capes and discothèque white whore pants.

(And this is not about *hatred*, but comes from trying
to make a separation between living and dying elements
in the world, in poetry no less than any place else. The
results are similar in any field or area. The counter mag-
netisms I spoke of before.)

The separation, the hunting, for fresh natural experience, is the approach to the self, but further, is the key to
the move past the self, as if to become part of the forces
of nature, the creative "urge" which is Godliness. Black
people are strong for the reasons they are strong. Despite
what you think exists we, black people, are the spiritual
people, yes, caught here among sinister materialists. The
end of one epic is the chaos (anti-form) preceding (as
different families, races come around in different guises,
through the centuries) the new, the black man because
he is the spiritual must rise now into another phase of
humanity, one that we have prepared for in our futility
and desperation, that is we are consciously determined
to evolve, by any means necessary, in a way that Darwin
could make only vague reference to.

The black poetry in America is the poetry of the changing evolving peoples. The living beings, the relatives of
the most ancient men on earth. Our feeling and understanding began at the beginning of the planet, and we
rise understanding this, and our songs, our images, go
from there to here. There are no mists over the African
Empires. The obscuration of our world has ended, We're
here again.

The black poetry is at extremes, where the most feeling
is. Are you being beaten in the streets? Is your whole life
to be a death trap or maybe you'll just end up framed for
dope charges by some hopelessly limited organism . . .

or your father, is he a man, has he been able to be, what
is your future, black poet, where are you, what will happen when the deal goes down, *Whatever deal* . . . do
you own your own energy?

American poetry, &c. anthologies are like memberships
in the same ofay suburban social clubs of the walkaround
world. We are poets from different sources, finally, for
different reasons. Only LeRoi Jones in New American
Poetry, 1945–60. *The* Negro! Whose poetry then, only a
reflection of what the rest of that E-X-C-L-U-S-I-V-E club
was doing. You mean there was no other poetry, you mean
there were no other spooks, &c. I pass.

From these different places in America, from whence
come these different voices, the black poetry is *the* different voice. It is, for the covered up artifactionists, not
poetry, not art, at all. Because ART is, "Well, let's face it,
something only white folks can do," except this is a society that does not even have a place for art in it, of any
kind.

The girlish professors cannot admit of anything as art
that would show that they are girlish professors. Just as
they cannot be in a place where Duke, Monk, JellyRoll,
Bird, Sun-Ra, or James Brown were Masters, or where
Shakespeare's "rhythm" was stale and punkish.

The black poet's blues and bebop, his "new thing," his
black music, are like Scott Joplin teaching mozart what
a cadenza really was, wit'out even being named or finally
resting (with that lil' bit a shit) there. And Rag was formal and written.

But listen to David Henderson make a wordclassic out
of The Impressions "Keep On Pushing," just as it was a
music classic . . . or Calvin Hernton or Charles Patterson turn the names of Harlem streets into the actual sweet
black furiousness of flailing nigger rhythm. Listen to Ron-
ald Stone make Charlie Parker's children words, and add
word music plainly together readmitting the simple chang-

ing heartbeat into "poetry." (Can Robert Lowell scat???)
LISTEN.

SOUND.

The word *sound*-ed, in its quicker leap from the mind,
as the cry or dancer, singer does, Making the voice leap
past the machine. (Past the formality of "literature,"
which is a cracked white vahz, nutty ol ladies think is
valuable.)

And these are a skittering of the new, but even so let
the names flow . . . we are young masters, Roland Snel-
lings, Lorenzo Thomas, Larry Neal, Ishmael Reed, William Kgositsile, Steven Young, A.B. Spellman, K.C., Bob
Kaufman, Allen Polite, Tom Postell, William Patterson,
Welton Smith, Hart LeRoi Bibbs what are we talking about
anyway . . . names?

(Frank Lima, wherever
you are, lookout young chico they'll turn you into a lady.)
Have you ever heard John Moore speak?

The reconstitution of *A Poetry* is in all areas, fields.
Poetry is of a people. One people or another. It tells about
their lives, it describes their worlds. The world we black
poets are making is for the new peoples, the growing, the
vital, the heroic in the face of, the pure lyric, song above
horror, or horror music of the place we are at, or the peace
we manage somehow to find, if we know about the godly
evolution of life, when it all is refined into spirit.

The people the black poetry speaks of are forerunners
and descendants of the inheritors, the spirit people. The
First ("primitive") and next "modern" phase.

The Nation rises.

Diplomat Magazine, June 1966

(For the old father divine lady with the street candy store)

November 1966:
One Year Eight Months Later

How long ago was Malcolm killed?* Days, years, months? It's hard to remember. So much has happened, so many changes, and diversions. New aspects. But always, it seems now, along a similar kind of direction. Allegiances entered into and broken, to be reassembled, other places.

Malik was the surge at one point and his relationship to the Nation Of Islam is as graphic a picture of world spirit as exists. And his break, into a secular (political) intelligence, understanding. His murder rendered most of the things directly associated with him into ruin. His, finally, was an abstract energy, a symbolizing of certain times of certain spirit. He was murdered because he summed up the whole black-white struggle in America,

* February 21, 1965.

and the world, too easily. He has risen, in a wide arc-circle to embrace a whole of public consciousness. He was pimp-prisoner, student-monk, firebrand-wiseman, and martyr. In each place his spirit settled, something was turned on, and over. A beginning, an ending.

We are now in a deep period of reaction. And it is late fall, toward winter, in America, and the Black People, white people think, can be more easily handled since cold is not their stick. Their energy seems to break out in those "long hot summers," and now with the cold, the civil rights bill is struck down. Which is symbol more than reality. Though the reality of its symbolization is real, and deadly. The bill never meant anything except one kind of promise. Nothing was to be done. But now, even the promise is swept away. There is talk of backlash. But it was frontlash, and coming back to get more meat on the next turn around. They hated Black People anyway.

It is like "The Redemption Of The South" in the 1870's when the Reconstruction promise was killed. Native so-cialisms, Black Suffrage and Power were swept away. Just as there is an attempt to sweep them away now. To stem the tide of Black insistence and will. The new Booker T.'s have come more clearly and insistently, damningly, to the front. Roy Wilkins, A. Philip Randolph, Bayard Rustin, Whitney Young, and the others, (and The Rev. King, him-self a little too slick to sign the death warrant* of young Black Hope which the others signed).

Since Malcolm's death Nkrumah has fallen, Sukarno has been tricked and put into burlesque captivity (McNa-mara admits this last "triumph" on tv before the sen-ators). These were two giants; add them to Malik. See the hideous loss, to any good. Though it is probably their own defects and errors that brought them down, as it is in *all* of our cases. But to be open or prone to certain in-jury or loss of energy, however it is projected, is defect and error. In one sense. Past the physical the spiritual

* Ad in NY Times repudiating Black Power.

takes over. And the progress moves into another level. There is constant universal "compensation." It is a "rule."

In domestic (US) politics, what is called backlash is a graphic metaphor of white thinking throughout the society, and nation. "Negroes are responsible for the Civil Rights Bill failing to pass. White People would no longer stand for their rioting and growing penchant for violent displays of self justification" (and despair), is the way it has been put more or less officially, governmentally, and by the walking around Daily Newses of America . . . and this "calm" speech is just a, the, slickveneer cover story for any angry white man afraid his shit is about to be stole.

The concept of Black Power is natural after Malcolm. Malcolm's legacy was the concept and will toward political power in the world for the Black Man. Just as the Muslims ask for land. Malcolm asked for World Power. Which is international, and speaks of nationhood, in whatever sense it is translated.

As Black Men we now understand that we can have nothing without power. Everyone should understand power tends toward the total, of being, the total. If I write President Johnson's speeches for him, he is dead in a week. Any power represents a total. So the asking for Black Power is the articulated primal cry. It could not mean simply "voting registration and electing sheriffs in counties which are 80% black." These are the simple garments of a more dazzling bid. Just as the thrust of Black Art was to free our images to disentangle them from the image(s) of the oppressor, so Black Power is the thrust of our total. We must have a world, too. "Look down, it is yours, these stores and houses, these hills and streams." We must have a part of this earth, now. We must build our own societies. As we have, Black Men, before, and before that, and even before that.

Malik taught (See "The Legacy of Malcolm X and The Coming of the Black Nation," *Home,* Wm. Morrow Pub-

lishers, 1966) that the Black Man must build his own
society, since he already had his own, separate, judgment
of what the world was, and how people ought to exist in
it. We must build a world according to *our* feelings. (The
white man cannot feel, otherwise he would feel the great
pain his presence causes in the world.) But we must build
these societies where we are, now. On the soil we have
helped cultivate, among the businesses and enterprises
we have built with the strength of our bodies and the for-
titude of our will. A society we have built in the strictest
of austerities: *slavery*.

Where we are, now. Which is Black Power. All our skills
must be turned toward our own. And we must build societies of the learned, the beautiful, the powerful. We are,
and will be, Spirit Worshipers. Worshipers of The Life
Process itself. This is our conflict with the West, with the
white man. He worships only things, and is willing in his
peculiar lust to sacrifice all of humanity for their bestial
aggrandizement.

But in the cyclical ebb and flow of human progress . . .
a final progress to spirit, and the totality of existence,
movement is one constant. It was absolute knowledge of
our environment, our total environment, that Malik gave
us. The absoluteness of the blackwhite struggle in the
world. The focus on that struggle, and its international
implications was the surge that Malik commanded. His
murder, not only critically ruptured American Black connections with the Third World, but crippled his own organization, and turned great numbers of Black People away
from The Nation Of Islam. There were no Black Nationalist or Black Revolutionary organizations that were not
affected. And that was exactly the point.

There have been many, are still many, attempts to take
on Malcolm's mantle, consciously and unconsciously
(which, in a sense, is how it should be). "He was our
manhood," as Ossie Davis stated so eloquently at the funeral service. But the most significant development since

Malcolm's assassination has been the emergence of the college aged Black Power spokesmen, headed by Stokely Carmichael, Director of SNCC.

The sudden leap to power within the organization by Carmichael and the other militants was not sudden at all. The black-white liasons that motivated many of the SNCC projects predominantly in the South were on shaky ground from the beginning. Malik made Black Nationalism an intelligent stance in our time, and many of the young SNCC workers were moved by Malcolm's image.

But Carmichael made it clear that from now on SNCC would wage a Black struggle. That the brains and will of the organization would be Black, like it or not. Which most of the white liberals associated with the various civil rights movements most certainly did not like. It marked a socio-political maturity and independence for a "civil rights" organization not found before. It also created an absolute split in the so called civil rights movement between the urgers of Tokenism . . . King, Wilkins, etal, and the genuine workers for Black independence.

The cries of Black Power swept through the nation. And with the approaching summer, and the increased volatility of the Black Man, even some of the "more conservative" civil rights leaders, and the whitethinking Negro journals edged over cautiously to make their own small claims of advocating Black Power in one form or another. "New," they said, but it was exactly the same things the Black leaders of the Reconstruction times were calling for after the Civil War. And with the recent defeat of the Civil Rights Bill, the soon to be passed "Riot Laws," the anti-Black Power statements by prominent whitethinking "Negro Leaders," and the general talk and tone of a White Backlash we are right back in the 1870's and the beginning of Jim Crow. What other kind of Crow they gonna run out now?

Added to these things, attempts to jail Stokely Carmichael, for "starting the Atlanta Riots," and cracker congress-

men's attempts to strip Adam Clayton Powell of his power,
and the New York branches attempts to put Powell, a Congressman, in jail, show that the white man is striking
back in his inimitable fashion.

With Viet-Nam always in the background, and growing
into the foreground of any talk about the United States
of America, it is not farfetched to make some conclusions
that the worldwide rage of reaction in Africa, Asia and
South America, coupled with the swift anti-Black moves
in domestic affairs (even the junking of great parts of
the Anti-Poverty program), and most of these things handled, directed, set-up and carried out by the United States
and its Smersh-Thrush-Spectre-like partner, the CIA, signals that perhaps Uncle Sap is planning a new, and larger
show for the world. Perhaps in the spirit of The Theater
Of Cruelty, Sheriff Johnson has a little revue getting ready
to go on the boards called *War With China.*

The Spirit of Malik, and its thrust, reoccurrence, obsti-
nate strengthening, have made any talk about foreign
wars shaky, even Viet-Nam, since an "unstable" Black
Man in the beast's belly means he can't shoot his best
shot at the rest of the world's peoples. So the white man
has been, and is now, readying his coldest stoppers for
any black agitators at home, so he can get ready for his
big job: The absolute destruction of human life on the
planet. Luckily there are too many of us colored people
in the world, and Beast will succeed in destroying only
his ugly self.

Onyx, 1966

What the Arts Need Now

What's needed now for "the arts" is to get them away from white people, as example of their "culture" (of their life, finally, and all its uses, e.g., art) and back where such strivings belong, as strong thrusts of a healthy people.

What we want now is plays of all instance. Filling in and extending so called "reality." Commenting, altering, rebutting it. But the same cause. Life.

Plays of specific finding. Plays of human occasion. That is, where is the confrontation (between life and "death"), the wrench of soul and white shit, ugliest. Bring in the image of man, and evolution triumphant again. Animals need humanism. The humans we will show embracing spiritism.

We will have plays for city hall. At the time of city hall. So black humanity will know how we lived. How we triumphed. Plays enabling Black People to stop bogus so-

called urban renewal, which be nigger removal, and the
repeated disarming of Carthage. But at the time of, and
at the place of. In the street, at the spot where such disarming is taking place. Have your actors shoot mayors if
necessary, right in the actual mayor's chambers. Let him
feel the malice of the just. Let the people see justice work
out repeatedly. Examples. Explain evolution.

Plays for the police department. Jew plays, whether con
rolling big ass communications or laying in southorange-
avenue always dough producing swamps. Light in every
element. Show the chains. Let them see the chains as
object and subject, and let them see the chains fall away.

We will place and strike according to the otone, or
"reality," and project our truth, our findings, as an action,
as a projection, into place, feeling, invisibility, of the
actual. This is to say that we are ghosts, too. But everything is a ghost.

Whore plays, black politician plays, plays of the instant
of silence in the shoeshine parlor. A whole, looking for a
whole. An ascendancy. An appearance. To break heads,
and tear down buildings.

We want a post-American form. An afterwhiteness
color to live and re-erect the strength of the primitive.
(Plays where history is absolutely meaningful and contemporary.) The first learnings of man. While we fly into
the next epoch.

Negro Digest, April 1967

The World You're Talking About

The sensitive collect and carry. What they do with these things are Beauty, illusion, delusion, good jobs in the city, vast empires or jars full of smoke. What ever they want. What they've seen or been seen as, their various lives. The different things that made them want to end those same variously.

The Black Poetry is a sensitivity to the world total, to the American Total. It is *about,* or *is* feeling(s). Even governmental structures are made the way people *feel* they should be made. The animating intelligence is a total of all existence. The many registrations. Ways of making sense, of sensing, the reactors, the midget di-dah lights glows wetnesses meaning. Worlds. Spectrums. Galaxies. What the god knows.

The Black Poetry deals with the spirit. I've said, "We are human knowing spirit." Our reach, our walk, our animation past our selves standing mute on the block before the iceman's trigger. Whatever our "techniques," we are, our lives demand that we be, humanists. So our content is literally about a world of humans and their paths and forms.

The Beatles can sing "We all live in a yellow submarine" because that is literally where they, and all their people (would like to) live. In the solipsistic pink and white nightmare of "the special life," the artifactbeings worshiping their smells frozen in glass and gaudy jewelry.

But we are on the streets, we are somewhere in the world. We are made by, see all sides, strive for rightness righteousness may it be the purity of the perfect description, so that even the blood boils through our words they describe, and are, (so well) a life function.

David Henderson's poetry is the world echo, with the strength and if you are conscious, beauty of the place tone. Out of the "privacy" of experience, any experience, rendered to the whole, with reference to the living, evolving, organism. In this case the black man longing for god who is him self, as are the other selves, who reach from and through the spiritual principle, shedding those "selves" to become the spirit of everything.

These are local epics with the breadth that the emotional consciousness of a culture can make. David Henderson is conscious, though it does not make him hover bodily but spiritually, he is no lighter-than-air attachment to the race. He is their magic thrust. Their attainment. Only god could say:

> "and Spenser
> because he had a hit record (moneywise not his)
> sported his long red conk all over Tin Pan Alley
> haranguing the Brill Building and shit . . .
> borrowing the single axled Cadillac
> by day
> to return at night

hair out of gas car out of gas
spent"

Bantu artists knew that they were the vessel of God.
"Good" and "Beautiful" were synonymous. The spirit of
everything. I understand this is the world you're talking
about Mr. Henderson. Bless you for it.

Introduction to *Felix of the Silent Forest*
by David Henderson

The Need for a Cultural Base to Civil Rites & Bpower Mooments

he civilrighter is usually an american, otherwise he would know, if he is colored, that that concept is meaningless fantasy. Slaves have no civil rights. On the other hand, even integration is into the mobile butcher shop of the devil's mind. To be an american, one must be a murderer. A white murderer of colored people. Anywhere on the planet. The colored people, negroes, who are Americans, and there are plenty, are only colored on their skin. They are white murderers of colored people. Themselves were the first to be murdered by them; in order to qualify.

The blackpower seeker, if connected to civilrights mooment can be bourgeois meaning. He wants the same civilrights/power white people have. He wants to be a capitalist, a live-gooder, and a deathfreak. In whatever

order. There is the difference Frantz Fanon implies in
BlkSkin-WhiteMask. Black Bourgeoisie can be white or
black. The difference is critical only if Black Black Bourgeoisie can be used for good, possibly. White ones are
examples of shadow worship, and are deathfreaks and
American.

Black Power cannot mean ONLY a black sheriff in the
sovereign state of Alabama. But that is a start, a road, a
conceptualizing on heavier bizness. Black Power, the
power to control our lives ourselves. All of our lives. Our
laws. Our culture. Our children. Their lives. Our total
consciousness, black oriented. We do not speak of the
need to live in peace or universal humanity, since we are
peaceful humanists seeking the spiritual resolution of the
world. The unity of all men will come with the evolution
of the species that recognizes the need for such. The black
man does. The black man is a spirit worshiper as well.
The religious-science and scientific-religion is the black
man's special evolutional province. He will reorder the
world, as he finds his own rightful place in it. The world
will be reordered by the black man's finding such place.
Such place is, itself, the reordering. Black Power. Power
of the majority is what is meant. The actual majority in
the world of colored people.

Census

BLACK PEOPLE BLACK PEOPLE BLACK PEOPLE
YELLOW PEOPLE YELLOW PEOPLE YELLOW
        PEOPLE
BROWN PEOPLE BROWN PEOPLE BROWN
RED PEOPLE RED PEOPLE RED PEOPLE
POOR PEOPLE POOR PEOPLE POOR PEOPLE
POOR PEOPLE POOR PEOPLE POOR PEOPLE
        POOR PEOPLE . . . . . .

& others.

Bourgeois black power seeks mostly to get in on what's
going down now. The implication or murderermembership

is clear. Of course the form of Bourgeois black power can be harnessed for heavier ends. The control by black people for their own benefit CAN BE set up similar to bourgeois black power, but if the ends are actually to be realized, you are talking again about nationalism, nationalization. Finally the only black power that can exist is that established by black nationalism. We want power to control our lives, as separate from what americans, white and white-oriented people, want to do with their lives. That simple. We ain't with yuall. Otherwise you are talking tricknology and lieconjuring. Black power cannot exist WITHIN white power. One or the other. There can only be one or the other. They might exist side by side as separate entities, but never in the same space. Never. They are mutually exclusive.

"Might exist," because that is theoretically possible, except the devils never want to tolerate any power but their own. In such cases they want to destroy what is not them. However, the power of the majority on the planet will exist, this is an evolutionary fact. The adjustment, what the world must go through because of this, is current events.

The socio-political workers for black power must realize this last fact. That the black and white can never come to exist as equals within the same space. Side by side perhaps, if the devils are cool, but the definition of **devil is** something uncool.

This means that any agitation within the same space for Black Power is for control of the space you *can* control called part of the society, but in reality in black enclaves, cities, land, where black people are usually already in control in terms of population. Further control must be nationalization, separation. Black power cannot exist except as itself, power, to order, to control, to legalize, to define. There are wars going on now to stop black power, whether in Sinai, Vietnam, Angola, or Newark, New Jersey. The difference is that in Newark, New Jersey, many colored people do not even *know* they are in this war (tho they might realize, on whatever level of consciousness, that they are losing).

Black power is nationalization. Absolute control of resources beneficial to a national group. It cannot come to exist in areas of white control. Neither Harlem nor Hough nor Watts &c. are really America. They are controlled by America . . . this is the sickness. Black power is the cure for this sickness. But it must be the alternative to what already exists, i.e., white power. And to be an actual alternative it must be complete.

Black power cannot be complete unless it is the total reflection of black people. Black power must be spiritually, emotionally, and historically in tune with black people, as well as serving their economic and political ends. To be absolutely in tune, the seekers of black power must know what it is they seek. They must know what is this power-culture alternative through which they bring to focus the world's energies. They must have an understanding and grounding in the cultural consciousness of the nation they seek to bring to power. And this is what is being done, bringing to power a nation that has been weak and despised for 400 years.

That is, to provide the alternative, the new, the needed strength for this nation, they must proceed by utilizing the complete cultural consciousness of this black nation's people. We should not cry black power unless we know what that signifies. We must know full well what it is we are replacing white power with, in all its implications. We are replacing not only a white sheriff, for the values that sheriff carries with him are, in fact, an extension of the white culture. *That black sheriff had better be an extension of black culture, or there is NoChange!* (In the sense that Edward Brooke, so-called Negro Senator from Massachusetts, as a representative of white culture, could never signify, in any sense, Black Power. He is, for all intents and purposes, a white man.)

There are people who might cry BlackPower, who are representatives, extensions of white culture. So-called BlackPower advocates who are mozartfreaks or Rolling Stones, or hypnotized by Joyce or Hemingway or Frank Sinatra, are representatives, extensions, of white culture, and can never therefore signify black power. Black power, as black, must be, is in reality, the total realization of that nation's existence on this planet from the year one until this moment. All those experiences which have been this lost nation's must be brought to bear upon all its righteous workings; especially for Power. (And with Power will come Freedom.) Black Power is the Power first to be Black. It is better, in America, to be white. So we leave America, or we never even go there. (It could be twelve miles from New York City (or two miles) and it would be the black nation you found yourself in. That's where yourself was, all the time.)

The very failure of the civil rights and blackpower organizations (collecting memberships on strictly sociopolitical grounds) to draw more membership is due to the fact that these organizations make very little reference to the totality of black culture. The reason Mr. Muhammad's Nation of Islam has had such success gathering black people from the grass roots is that Mr. Muhammad offers a program that reflects a totality of black consciousness. Islam is a form of spirit worship (a moral guide) as well as a socio-economic and political program. Religion as the total definer of the world. (This is as old as the world, and finally will be the only Renewal possible for any of us to submit to the Scientific-Religious reordering of the world, through black eyes and black minds.) It must be a culture, a way of feeling, a way of living, that is replaced with a culture, feeling, way of living and being, that is black, and, yes, finally, more admirable.

Hence, the socio-political must be wedded to the cultural. The socio-political must be a righteous extension of the cultural, as it is, legitimately, with National groups.

The american negro's culture, as it is, is a diphthong with
the distortions of the master's hand always in back or
front ground, not real but absolutely concrete and there;
. . . the culture, the deepest black and the theoretical
. . . socio-politico (and art &c.) must be wedded. A culturally aware black politics would use all the symbols of
the culture, all the keys and images out of the black past,
out of the black present, to gather the people to it, and
energize itself with their strivings at conscious blackness.
The Wedding . . . the conscious-unconscious. The politics and the art and the religion all must be black. The
social system. The entirety of the projection. Black Power
must mean a black people with a past clear back to the
beginning of the planet, channeling the roaring energies
of black to revive black power. If you can dig it??? Not to
discover it now . . . but to revive. Our actual renaissance
(Like the devils pulled themselves out of their "dark ages"
by re-embracing the "classics," or Classicism: what they
could see as the strengths and beauties of a certain kind
of "pure" Europeanism (whiteness). And with that went
to the source! Eastern Thought . . . black african-middle
eastern, also the re-embracing of the Far East via Marco
Polo, &c., like Trade).

So that no man can be "cultured" without being *consciously* Black. Which is what we're talking about all the
time, in any Rising (Evolutional) Pitch. *Consciousness*.

The Civil Righters are not talking about exchanging a
culture. They are, no matter what moves they make, layin'
in the same place, making out. Black Power, as an actuality, will only exist in a Black-oriented Black-controlled
space. It is White Culture that rules us with White Guns.
Our only freedom will be in bringing a Black Culture to
Power. We Cannot Do This Unless We Are Cultured. That
is, Consciously Black. (The Consciousness of Black Consciousness must know & Show itself as well.)

The erection of large schools teaching Black Consciousness. Wherever there are Black People in America. This

should be one definite earnest commitment of any Black
Power group. Even the rundown schools full of black children deep in the ghettos are white schools. The children
are taught to value white things more than themselves. All
of them are white-controlled, and the quality of education
suffers because white people want the quality of our education to suffer, otherwise something else would be the
case. We will have no quality education for our children
until we administer it ourselves. You *must* know this!

There is no black power without blackness conscious of
itself. "Negro History" is not what we must mean, but the
absolute reordering of our Education Systems. In other
words, the philosophy of blackness, the true consciousness
of our world, is what is to be taught. The understanding
of the world as felt and analyzed by men and women of
soul.

The Black Student Union of San Francisco State College has started moving toward a "Black Studies Program"
at that school. A Black Studies Program on departmental
status at the school, where students could spend all of
their time re-creating our black past, and understanding,
and creating the new strong black nation we all must
swear to bring into existence.

The black power groups must help to create the consciousness of who we black people are, and then we will
be driven to take power, and be faithful to our energies as
black people with black minds and hearts, quite a *different*
people from the species that now rules us.

Afro-American History, African History, Realistic World
History, Eastern Philosophies-Religion, Islam-Arabic-Afri-
can Religion and Languages, Black Art-past and contem-
porary, The Evolving Patterns of the Colored World, Black
Psychology, Revolutionary Consciousness, Socio-Political
Evolution of Afro-Americans, Africans, Colored Peoples,
War, The Placement of the New Culture, Eastern Science,
Black Science, Community Workshops (How To) in Black
Power, Business and Economics: Keys to a new black

world, given the strengths our studies into times of the black man's power will build for us. Black Studies is to make us cultured, i.e., consciously black.

The so-called Negro Colleges ought to be the first to be forced into Blackness. The consciousness of the self, without which no righteous progress is possible. Instead the Negro Colleges are "freak factories," places where black children are turned into white-oriented schizophrenic freaks of a dying society. But many of the students have already shown that they are not willing to be misused by the whiteminds of their puppet professors.

A cultural base, a black base, is the completeness the black power movement must have. We must understand that we are *Replacing* a dying culture, and we must be prepared to do this, and be absolutely conscious of what we are replacing it with.

We are sons and daughters of the most ancient societies on this planet. The reordering of the world that we are moving toward cannot come unless we are completely aware of this fact, and are prepared to make use of it in our day-to-day struggle with the devil.

E.G.: Black Art—The re-creation of our lives, as black . . . to inspire, educate, delight and move black people.

It is easier to get people into a consciousness of black power, what it is, by emotional example than through dialectical lecture. Black people seeing the re-creation of their lives are struck by what is wrong or missing in them.

Programmatic application of what is learned through black art is centrally the black power movement's commitment.

The teaching of colored people's languages, including the ones we speak automatically, moves the student's mind to other psychological horizons. European language carries the bias of its inventors & users. *You must be* anti-black, speaking in their language, except by violent effort. The masses of black people, for instance, have never spoken the European's languages. Or let me say, they have never spoken them to such degree that the complete bias of that "competence" would dull their natural tuning.

The teaching of Black History (African and African-American) would put our people absolutely in touch with themselves as a nation, and with the reality of their situation. You want them to move to take power, they must know how they can deserve this power.

Black Power must be a program of Consciousness. The consciousness to Act. (Maulana Ron Karenga and the US organization in Los Angeles work very successfully at making black consciousness cultural and of course sociopolitical.) It should all be one thing. Blackness.

Voting nor picketing nor for that matter fighting in the streets means anything unless it is proposed by a black consciousness for the aggrandizement and security of the Black culture and Black People. Each of our "acts of liberation" must involve the liberation of the Black man in every way imaginable.

Black Power movements not grounded in Black culture cannot move beyond the boundaries of Western thought. The paramount value of Western thought is the security and expansion of Western culture. Black Power is inimical to Western culture as it has manifested itself within black and colored majority areas anywhere on this planet. Western culture is and has been destructive to Colored People all over the world. No movement shaped or contained by Western culture will ever benefit Black people. Black power must be the actual force and beauty and wisdom of Blackness . . . reordering the world.

The Black Power Revolt, 1967

From: The Book of Life

Newark St. years later—
Dante vanished, a Black Man in his place. Beaten, for a
time. Humbled, for a time. This time to be given to
strengthening and wisening. Blackening. To the first virtues. The first virtue, which is Blackness!

But all virtues are virtues of the heart. Let the head
profit from the heart and no other. Let the signs that God-
Allah shows be answered by our obedience.

In the darkness the moon will shine upon the signs.
The red lights will show clearly in the darkness, and the
heartily fortified will prosper. The ignorant, the unworthy,
the mere "thinkers" will surely perish.

The leaders of Black People . . . Black People where
will you find them? But in yourselves, of your selves. The
wise, the loving, the strong, the heroic! Make no mistake.
Your leaders are your selves. The Black Hearted!

If knowledge were
anything
it could not
(be) but
matter
The vibration
The heart's pulse
In the instant
all is transformed
Great Cities erected
in a waste land

Say only what you know
Clearly & freely & swiftly, as it comes
Springing from
the heart!/ This will be

true

if truth can

exist

This will be beautiful

if there is

such

You will go where you lead yrselves, and only when
you lead yrselves. Strong wise charitable loving. Feeling
the earth moon and stars. The natural flow of life force—
from spirit to spirit. We are the universal energy trans-
forming itself. Allah Krishna Chakra Obatala Vowels of
Life. The thousand names of Divinity. Ism-Al-Azam!

So be it the Black Man must learn himself. Relearn
who he is. His origins. His powers. His destiny. His power

will be reforged in fire. Actual flame, like a star bursting
into a million worlds!

There are many conscious Black men walking this
planet. As there have been since the first men. Our knowledge stretches from the beginning of the planet. Believe
this, Brother, and lift up yr self!

We are creators, the first to walk the earth. Allah-God
made Black Man first. Our color is what the closest substance to the sun would be. Thoroughly fashioned in the
heat of passionate creation. Blackness we worship thee!
Our supreme identification.

All beings come from Allah-God. All beings are the
consciousness of Allah-God. There is nothing except it
ride the energies of all creation. Part of the Whole.
The yellow races are a median, hence their numbers, and
all but persistent strength (From Kubla Khan to Mao Tse-
Tung). The white races are a last raw turn before the
stretching and reaching of return recycle evolutionary
movement Black.

"The circle complete" to Black, back to Black, "first and
first and first" (identifying the spinning, the cycles, of
birth. death. rebirth ☉

Devils are devils because they need to be devils to exist
at all. They are opposites necessary for change. The math-
ematics of creation (at one level). We rise past devils,
past *that* resistance (as in electrical talk, the same physical principles). Heat and light from burning dumb matter. Devils are fuel for the flames of righteousness!

Dear Wife

Dear Son (also my daughters)

Life Life LIFE is what we want. We want life more desperately than anyone. But where is it? There is no life without *honor!*

We must choose the way we live. Under what laws and under what Gods! Our rule will be just . . . because we *feel* (the need for) justice (dear wife you taught me) we understand the demand all Allah-God's creatures make for justice.

It is time for Beauty and Truth to rule the world again. It is time for the evolved beings to reorder this planet.

Year 1967 A.D. (by this measure). We have been away from home 400 years. We are still in bondage O, Allah, O, Shango . . . We know it is yr will but we are weak flesh and cannot understand as you understand . . . past infinity (and back). But we begin now to long for ourselves and for your wisdom, which is the light of ourselves. We know we have been judged harshly, but we begin now to understand that this is the judgment to burn away an old dumb flesh . . . burn away the veils from our eyes so that we will see the newness of our re-creation. O Allah O Shango (rulers of our ancient cities) O Osiris, we will be closer to you from now on. We will work only through the divine light of your righteous energy.

The war on the devil has begun throughout this land! We begin to feel ourselves again, and know the passion of righteous action.

We are not murderers. We have oppressed no man. We seek only to rule ourselves under the divine will of (Allah

and Shango) our Beings. We will Live! We will yet rebuild
our noble cities, and use the planet's resources in our
natural way.

Gold is to wear or build with—(diamonds rubies pearls)
not to be valued as more than men. The natural scale of
evolutional value is understood by the natural (Black)
man. Minerals are lowest in the evolutional scale. A man
is higher than mineral vegetable or animal. A man has
the capacity to evolve into his soul's spirit, as a spirit
being. We have a living expanding Holy essence.
The essence of our creator

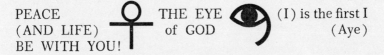

PEACE   THE EYE   (I) is the first I
(AND LIFE)   of GOD   (Aye)
BE WITH YOU!

The Ancient Egyptians are still in chains. "Lay On
Symbol." We will yet be ourselves again. The prophets
walk among us. The Heroes. The men of God. Listen to
Goodness and you can be Goodness, P+S+L are among
us now, in the meanest of circumstances . . . preaching
and trying to awaken us. Listen!

Gentle singer of songs must *scream* down the bastions
of Evil. Reflecting Scientist must discover the tools that
we need to be free! All must be harnessed. All love all
energy all passion must be harnessed and directed so that
we may all re-enter the city of God!

The city is burning! The Devil's city is in flame! And
because evil beings have tortured our people by worshiping dumb objects more than human life, our people run

through the streets with these objects. Sometimes they are
murdered. But also they run with what they need smash-
ing and destroying the temples of the UnGodly. Temples
where evil beings sell our people things and keep them
chained to illusions of Desire.

Pop pow pow Boom!! The flame The flame. Red shadows moving near the darkness. Devils whirling round and
round, frightened that God is near and their deaths are
imminent!

Our people dance in the street now! Young men and
old men. Arms full. Little girls outfitting their hovels with
what they've learned to desire on television. Dancing In
The Street!!

On the roofs the marksmen of Shango and Allah look
down and judge the dancers. A devil whirls into the
flames, a new eye blind in the center of his skull! Allahu
Akbar!

Devils whiz by afraid of the dancers! Those whom the
devil has tortured with dope smash the temples of drugs.
Shoe stores burn false discounts and corn making oxfords!
Poison wine bubbles behind hot broken glass. The most
"precious" beverages fly through the night with the
Brothers.

Pop! pop! pop! Crowds wheeling breaking standing and
laughing fleeing the devil's screaming red eye.

Doom to the devil total death will come soon Doom
Doom to the Devil. Young armies of God reformed after
400 years attacking with the most natural of weapons
holding against the scourges of Satan our honor our lives
our holy Blackness!

When the devils catch a dancer they murder him at
once or else they throw the single human to the earth and
stomp and beat him with sticks and try to break his bones
and tear out his privates (in terrible envy) and scream
"Animals Animals Animals," describing only themselves
in their frenzy. Not understanding the human they are

trying to murder grows stronger and stronger than ever before. ALL PRAISES TO THE BLACK MAN!

—Essex County Jail
Summer   1967
Year of Rebellion

This essay was written shortly after the rebellion of 1967. It was submitted to Atlantic & *several other periodicals but turned down. Most of its accusations have now, of course, proven out. Like Addonizio, Spina &c. indictments. And now, since the 1970 election the title seems truly prophetic!*

Imamu Baraka, 1970

Newark—
Before Black Men Conquered

A. The city of Newark is the sun object projected, magnified, actually blown-up, with hard guns smacking through night. Killing niggers up and down the streets. Breaking pictures of Jesus. Humbling a people to Allah.

The first night rumors. In the heat of the broke down city. Nobody could live in Newark without being stretched out through the final circus colors of America & alienated, No, not even in any America, except the real one!

The common terror of Newark is its spooky absence of any advertised American ideal. Except it is exactly what America is. A sham of ugliness. A sham gesture of humanity, except where strong black life exists and lights up the righteousness and danger to righteousness.

Black People in Newark are strong. They only need to *KNOW IT*. And ACT on it!

Black People in Newark are more than 63% of the listed
resident population. And probably closer to 75% of the
people who actually *live* in the city *all the time*. Central
Newark is totally black except a light fringe of PR* which
trails off from High cross South Broad swelling again S.E.
down Neck.

Clinton Hill, once Jewish now Black. North of Sussex and
down across Clifton to Broad once Wop, now Black with
the compliment of Latin. North Newark and way across
pushing to Weequahic Ave. now Black: pressing the few
Jews in pork panic their backs against Hillside and the
newly American park. (I remember many years ago Dr.
Burch was the first family up the slope of Meeker Ave.
"The Good Parts." Quiet Weequahic, once Jewheaven now
is Route 66 of Black desire. And down on Bergen & Custer,
where used to be gefillte fishes for asswipe, bees now
Home of The Brave Willie, harder and newer and aimin'
to kick *somebody's* ass.

One of our small capitols is near those streets. One of
our centers. Fat Nigger Police hang out in some spots,
collars open sweating and being corny bigshots of a dying
world.

Swift Hawthorne Ave. & Berrrrr-gin??

(They stoned devils on Bergen like they was goin outta
style! Mu-tha-fuckin JewAss Peedabed cocksucka!!!! Bam-
Bam—they tore up a piece a sidewalk to throw at one
dude and a beast lady wheeled her car to get off Springfield or some shit and almost turned the short over
wheelin straight into the 12Foot Ants.)

Junk City moved South too, in the good section, there's
trees. A remnant of The Jews. Also in that section, Lee
Bernstein, "A councilman for all the people," just as Hugh
Addonizio is "A Mayor For All The People." Bernstein and
Addonizio have Nigger STOOGES run around and grin
at folks and promise anything unemotional!

Bernstein and Addonizio got in because Negroes were

* 10% of total population.

divided and sold out. As usual. Black People will not be divided! Bernstein because Bill Payne, who was Kennedy image Negro (*was* because hopefully his tv speech on how bayonets were thrust through his window and his knowing, in her last hours, Mrs. Eloise Spellman, mother of 11 children whom devil soldiers blasted through the windows of the jail they had her living in . . . might indicate he's trying to get some soul), and Earl Harris,* an Adamish mature slickster; a Black Republican, fought each other for the South Ward and Bernstein,† who is not even really jew-slick, eased back on in.

Payne and Harris supposedly had agreed before to accept the findings of other Negroes as to which one was better equipped to run . . . so the Councilmanic spot would be Black to represent Black. However they did not hold with such agreement and each ran and each lost. All Black People lost, even those couple who showed up grinning on Bernstein's posters saying "Buy White"!

Addonizio . . . because the ugly Toms he marshals, beat or promised or harassed Negroes into division and left the one Black mayor candidate, Ken Gibson,‡ off in a full lurch that neither Dick Gregory nor Martin Luther King could overcome.

The Mayor-Councilmanic election in 1966 was fantasy on the real side. George Richardson's headquarters are broken into and stuff thrown all over. Independent Black Mayoral candidate Kenneth Gibson's posters and flyers were ripped down or painted black. And Italian Rat Drawings of Gibson began to appear up and down the avenues. (After the rebellion Irish Carey, County Chairman . . . the unwholesome Spencer Tracy of our lives . . . has named Richardson to run on the Reg. Dem Ticket, in a

* Now Councilman-at-large, 1970.

† Recalled in 1969 by Richardson backed Rev. Horace Sharper. who then lost in 1970 to Community Choice candidate for south ward councilman, Sharpe James.

‡ Became mayor, running as "The Community's Choice" in June 16, run-off election, 1970.

futile coolout motion, not wanting Richardson's* Freedom
Ticket to remount. And if it doesn't remount it never
existed anyway!)

Away from and deep in America, men threaten black
candidates and the Italian candidate a Mayor for all the
people is making sure that all the people that do not understand that he is for all the people will understand one
way or another. (The Italians understand that Addonizio
is for all the people. The Jews know that Bernstein is for
all the people . . . even in his vicious attacks on the
local anti-poverty agency . . . demanding that it be controlled by city officials . . . all of whom have a direct
connection with poverty . . . *Enforcing It!*) Only the
honest Black candidates are not for all the people . . .
they are just for most of the people.

Councilman Frank Addonizio, the Mayor's cousin, is for
all the people too. He said in a recent meeting where there
were mostly Black People (like the city itself) and Negroes
in the audience, that he "could stack the audience too." I
guess he meant like he and his brother have stacked most
of the city hall jobs with Italians. Tho in a straight out
breakdown as to who could stack what, in an open call,
it seems mathematically incorrect to figure he could stack
such meetings of *Newarkers* with more Italians, since
most of them do not live in Newark anymore. Especially
the ones with the goodies' jobs! But for sure he could stack
it with police and mafiosi.

The Addonizios, along with Police Director, Dominick
Spina (and their more soft spoken paisan Malafronte
. . . he a weak gesture in the direction of rationalism
. . .) run Newark with an iron foot. (Plus the gangsters.)
Their Irish step-brothers they have booted upstairs to
County bizness. But Nwk stuff is strictly Italian owned
and operated.

In the old days hard feelings between Black and Italian

---

* Richardson was paid divider in 1970 Community Choice Campaign. He got only 2000 votes in an ignominious defeat.

could always lead to minor brushfire war. On any corner
near the North ward. In 1947 a Black cat named Hailey,
in my 8th grade class, was shot down by two Ginnies for
winning too many foot races. There was a race riot following that incident that lasted, in a series of violent happen-
ings, more than a week. (One of the first cops to whip my
head during '67 rebellion was an Italian I knew from Barringer, where Italian language was part of the curriculum,
Detective Jerry Mellillo.)

And the Italians got Newark the way it's shown in the
Spencer Tracy picture that the Irish got Boston, by taking
it. Newark's owners understand force and power. Any
other approach they think of as weakness.

Carrying Addonizio's slop bucket and giving out free
samples to Black folks are quite a few handkerchief heads
. . . but the undisputed leaders are Councilman Calvin
West,* who was elected Councilman-at-large, riding in on
Addonizio's tail, and his sister, Larrie Stalks, the real
nigger-o representative in the Addonizio machine. She is
known in some circles as Madame Nhu.

Mrs. Stalks is a belly punchin Tomette Addonizio fol-
lower for the last 15 years. She began as his secretary
when he was in congress and has risen to undisputed
Chief Nigger slop ladeler for the regime. She now carries
the title "Director of Health & Welfare." † She once used
to shine shoes on Broad Street when she was a little boy,
and has shined her way clear to the top of the boots!

Mrs. Stalks is the "man" behind Mr. West, and actually
makes most of his decisions for him. Mr. West cam-
paigned in Newark also "for all the people," advocating a
new sports stadium and public first aid stations. He made
no real appeal to the Black community and was the only
nigger-o candidate to get any appreciable amount of white
votes.

* Defeated in 1970, and indicted w 'Addonizio and other mem-
bers of that council for extortion.
† Replaced in 1970.

(During the rebellion Mrs. Stalks and Mr. West were
out of town at an NAACP convention.)

The other Negro councilman is old line shuffler Irvine
Turner.* But shuffling Irvine was not always shuffling
Irvine. Anyway, not so completely so. The Honorable
Irvine Turner, the first Negro Councilman in Newark,
back in 1954. Mr. Turner's breakthrough into American
politics was made possible by getting into political shape
the Black Central Ward and establishing a leadership
category for Black People going for the Democratic party
tip. Some of Turner's lieutenants and associates like
Arthur Love, John Hicks, &c., in the mostly gangster
oriented Central Ward, were far more hoodish in their
heyday than they are in the now world, but they still like
to go for bad! But Italians always maintained control over
the pay-offs and the safer higher paying crime. As they do
today, on a nationwide level.

Now Irvine, who once seemed outspoken is screamed on
regularly as a Tom. Though he is a sick man in reality,
probably from the scummy air in Nwk City Hall, who just
barely knows where or who he is from day to day. Where
once he offered some actual inspiration to Black People
in Newark, now he represents the impotence and incom-
petence of one traditional area of Negro leadership. An
area of Negro leadership that once could boast that it
represented Black People.

Now Turner trails in the Addonizio jetstream by default
with pictures shaking hands with NoNeck and LBJ. "Re-
elect Dedicated Public Servant #12 Years Of Service #
First One Of His Race In America To Serve As Secretary
To Congressman Addonizio." That sounds like shit now.

The situation in a city of Black majority 1967 without
a single Black Captain on the police force. (Whoops! They
just made one!) The second largest insurance center in
America . . . the bus carries its workers into the city and

---

* Defeated in 1970 by Community's Choice candidate, Dennis
Westbrooks.

takes them and the bus back home to the suburbs. The merchandise sold in Newark has grown shoddier and shoddier, as the greys rushed to the suburbs. And the Springfield Ave. that just got busted was only a shadow of its former self. As Addonizio said after the rebellion, "The city is bankrupt." And now it is paying $800,000 to the police for beating and shooting Black heads, overtime. And of course, the majority of Newark's taxpayers (the most heavily taxed city in New Jersey) are Black. So then Black taxpayers are paying to get their homes shot up! Overtime!

Newark is a ghastly looking place all the time. Even before the out and out shooting war. (In fact it has never seemed as beautiful as it did those nights fire was eating up the sky.) It hangs broken in half with a ghost town—downtown in the center—and just above this ghost town the Central Ward: where Southern Black People fall off greyhounds everyday "too scared to go to Harlem."

Parts of the Ward look just like a rural southern town. People sit out in the street and eat and talk and drink and laugh. And everybody knows everybody from block to block.

Downtown is a ghost town after 5 because the Crackers live off somewhere WestOrange-SouthOrange-Teaneck-Montclair-Bloomfield-Maplewood, &c.&c. &c., a hundred suburbs dripping with money taken out of Newark. And the downtown's for white people in daylight, long gone by fingerpoppin night. There's almost nothing downtown for Black People. (But there'll be property and spots for the asking after the next phase of the rebellion.)

There is a clearer feeling in Newark, than any other city I have ever been in, of Colonialism. Newark is *a colony*. A bankrupt ugly colony, in the classic term, where white people make their money to take away with them. The city is kept up only as far as its money-making capacity, say for Prudential Life Insurance, &c. &c., &c.

The school system is almost non-existent. Schools are

horribly overcrowded, and 80-some percent of the school enrollment is black. And the schools are old and falling. They were old and falling 20 years ago when I passed through. (The coming school year even grammar school classes will start to double up in the so-called team system, though no Newark teachers have been instructed in that system. And they are trying to get the kids at Peshine Ave. school to go to school from 2 in the afternoon until 8:00 PM at night. Also, now 92 white teachers are resigning from Newark School system immediately and there's a "threat" that some 400 more are considering it. Boss! I say. Let us get our own! There are no Black principals.* There are only 2 (Whoops! 3) on The Board of Education, out of eleven, including one Italian who wanted teachers going to a Negro History seminar in Washington, D.C., docked.

Italian Barringer has a new building and one night had a 10 person lobby at the Bd of Ed meeting demanding a parking lot and a pool . . . when most schools in Newark dont even have enough classrooms. SouthSide High, whose Black enrollment is conservatively estimated at 99%, not only is falling down but there is talk that it is in danger of losing its accreditation. Central High, about 90% Black is in the same state, falling down even worse. The other high schools and grammar schools with high Black enrollment all look like death traps and are as old as the devil. Only Weequahic (which was once as Jewish as any *schul*) and Barringer, to a certain extent, have any learning school atmosphere. And even in those two schools uneasiness circulates the student blood as the Blood population increases. (Weequahic's all American basketball team is All Black.) And there have been fireworks not only between students but between teachers and students as they grapple with the dying culture.

Our children in most of these so called schools are not being taught anything. And when they are taught some-

* Since rebellion some have been named.

thing it is usually to hate themselves. (A teacher sends a pupil home to me from Central, "Catholics is the best religion and Stokely Carmichael, Adam Powell, and 'Cassius Clay' ain't no good!") The Jesuitical malice crowding down the larger streets and twisting and turning . . . till wait! Look!

There is St. Benedicts, almost all out of town Irish-Italian-Catholic. They have a new theater which plays stuff like *Oklahoma, Hello Dolly, Lil' Abner,* at the edge of the ghetto for same Irish-Italian audience. Except they did do *A Raisin In The Sun* after two months of 8 hour daily rehearsals, for an audience of nigger-o's in tuxedos and NoNeck and his boys, for $7.00 a haid. Lovely!

But Our Lady Queen of Angles on the Belmont Hill does a thriving bizness on Black folks with the same energetic inscrutability. They will soon be building, it's sd, a Center For The Performing Arts, with Fed money! And they work hard at what they do in the Black community because most of the big nigger-o churches are personal glory holes with suitable and appropriate psycho-dramas. (Some of the preachers slid around during the war with little "Cool It" signs made up for them personally by "God.")

The nigger-o churches have worked for nothing in the Black community, with a few exceptions,* but collections and Cadillacs. One beautiful exception is Rev. Sharper of Abyssinia Church who has always lent himself to the Black spirit of change.

The nigger-o ministers are, as usual, the worst Toms on the planet.† Like my man Rev. Benjamin Franklin Johnson (really!) who arose at the first Medical School hearing to say, "I wouldn't want to live in any all-colored city." I guess he couldn't anyway with the grey faggot he

---

* Among the growing list of exceptions are Rev. Cade, Central Presbyterian; Rev. Thomas, New Hope; Rev. Seward, Mt. Zion, Rev. Grant; Rev. Stephens.

† Again, since 1967, many exceptions in the growing black consciousness.

got hanging on the wall over he haid! Also he is about to
front a Kislak Co-op "for the people" at the Med School
site. It's a hundred and something rent . . . as BF Johnson said, "I'm not just talking . . . I'm doing something."
It is the B .F . Johnsons who will burn with the rest of the
dead wood, when this ol' city catchafire again!

NEGRO REMOVAL

Get to the tone of this place, this Black colony. Where
liquor stores close at 10, and they cant even sell beer on
Sunday. Except the Brothers bootleg, and even on Sunday
Official Jew sits open since before I was born selling
poison wine to the slaves, with detectives and uniformed
cops leaning on the boxes.

You can pay off anything in Newark, so completely
rotten and graft-ridden is the place. It is a graft oriented
city. A city of deals and kickbacks, and low low shit.

The Central Ward is old and beat up and junkie ridden
. . . and where they've torn the old buildings down
they've erected 13-story jails named after people the resi-
dents dont know. Tall dull red cells, really small towns in
themselves where the struggle is being plotted in earnest.

Hayes Homes, one of the oldest of these projects, was a
central target for the cops during the war. They shot
thousands of rounds into those ugly buildings. And at this
very moment workmen are scrambling around trying to
clean up the evidence of such cold beastthink. People talk
about crawling around the floor all night as the brave
police and guardsmen shot and shot into the buildings.
Many families crawled out into the halls to escape the
shattering glass and murderous lead barrage. The woman,
Mrs. Spellman, was killed looking out of her window in
Hayes Homes. Several days after the rebellion had been
declared officially over, they were still finding dead bodies
in Hayes, one of which was already starting to stink!

The Central Ward is Project City. At one point as you

stand on West Kinney Street all you can see in any direction are those long red jails, on all sides, full of dangerous
black people.

First to be herded into these cold tombs and then to be
sprayed with the lethality of barbarianism. But why all
these tombs, all these memorials to the sterility and failure of the white mind, and the slavery of the Black.

The plan is to get us all together. In one place, where
50 rolls of barbed wire could solve all the social dilemmas
these owners think are crucial. Who don't go in the projects must go somewhere. (The hypothesis.) They hope
out of town. But again crazy-ass greys assuming we are
they. We will simply turn the South Ward into a Central
Ward. The North, East and WestWards too. When the
next fire comes we will walk these streets with complete
impunity, and move in the empty stores.

But Negro Removal is the name of the game in Newark.
By any means necessary. They say the death toll, 26, is
phony. Where cops hang out the figure is put in the 40's,
the upper 40's. Rumors of hidden dead laying now till
they can be eased out, in Newark Morgue, and flying
around the black city.

Memories (and photographs) of James Rutledge, 19,
with 39 bullet holes in his split open corpse is the early
sleep image in a lot of Black People's minds. The constant
idiot roar of the scared police guns. Popping and popping
are still clogging Black People's ears. The pure white terrible evil jesuitical pall of murder is remembered darting
above all our heads. And the blood. The shot off faces and
breasts. The screams. The beatings. In this blood inquisi-
tion, we finally confess to you butcher priests that we are
Heretics. Yes, we are Black and We Will be free!

Negro Removal, by any means necessary. First the
Medical School is fresh in our minds. The edging in, the
final victory of money and malice over people is still on
the boards. The Lies. A mouth where his neck wd be, like

a pouting weasel, embarrassed by his naked head. Greasy
Liar. Says: I am for all the people.

The Medical School "controversy" set bloods boiling. It
was the light action preceding the actual knuckle drill.

The Medical School controversy as it's called in white
newspapers is just more Negro Removal but on the
(quasi) legal side. 155 acres they say they need for the
med school. I doubt that there is a Med School on the
planet that needs 155 acres! Some 23,000 Black folks wd
have to split behind this stuff too. To somewhere! Public
Housing Director Danzing insists there are places for all
these "Negroes" to move. Even he knows better. There is
a waiting list to get into Public Housing. And no matter
what they talked about "turn over," there is still a waiting
list. Now.

Also many Black People, myself included, see this med
school thing as a practical political move, a political act,
aimed at cutting through the potential strength of the
Ward, killing off the growing Black Power!

Black Power Black Power Black Power Black Power
Black Power! Dig It? It *Will* prevail!

Running the Black People out of town, Plus 3 highways
also scheduled to come through. The 16th District has
already been leveled and soon on up West Market Street
including a hundred year old baptist church, with a
framed bronze plaque to my Godfather in the lobby. No
Roman Catholic churches will be leveled. That God dont
have to leave for the highway, the med school or nothing
the fuck else!

But Black People need a Community College, a free
Community College so that our children can get into the
first part of so-called higher education. Black children by
and large will not be in any Med School in Newark,
though they will have to move out of the way for those
white people that will. And that is pure ugly bullshit, and
everybody knows it. (They are building a community college in Bloomfield, a distant extension of Naples.)

There have been meetin's and scream-ins so-called
blight hearings all "to determine whether or not the Medical School shd be put in the place designated." Certainly
the Greys have already decided where the Med School is
to go, (they told us!) and that it needs 155 acres (even
tho HUD agency says they only asked for 46). And that
these Black People have to get out, any way they can.
Most of the property is being "roughed off" in condemna-
tion proceedings, which is out and out fraud. The area
has not ever been officially designated a "Blighted Area."

A cold subfreezing wind blows between the Black and
white. Cave echoes. Arms in stroboscopic detail coming
down on heads. All in between. Do you understand what
slavery is? What the things that enslave must be?? And
we are told to talk to them. (We have.) Rationally. To!
God! Love them! This criminal blowing frozen shit blocks
any direct connection. We are separate and we have always been/separate. They ask if we are separatists. If we
want a separate state. We have always been separate
here. And wherever we were. Separate from them. You
ever hear of a ghetto? That's separate. A separate state.

But now we understand. A lot of us. That separate is
cool, is Right, is NATURAL. What we want is the power
to control that separate state. To control its politics and
its economics. The absolute power over *OUR* lives. *OUR*
lives. Get it? *Our Lives.* Over our children's lives and
education. Our employment. All the things that describe
and circumscribe men. We want to control. We want to
be ourselves . . . and benefit by it. Can you dig that?
And Benefit By It! All Praises Due To The Black Man!

To control it. To keep the money in our communities to
own and operate the businesses. To own and operate the
politicians, for our own benefit . . . not the dazzling
madness of self hatred double think "Massa, I'se here
killin' off my own folks agin" type Calvin West–Larrie
Stalks style to Roy Wilkins . . . To Control all Sayers
for and of Black.

What the "Med School Controversy" represents (and it
is still there, to be talked about already decided decisions)
is the attempted political murder of Black Power in Newark. This district they want to raze has a good percentage
of the registered Black voters and Black businesses. No-
mads cannot register. NoNeck wants in by remote control
in '70 through the sambo puppet, West. Addonizio himself
has visions of a beatified ascension through garlicky
golden clouds to GOVERNOR. (He wont make it He dont
have enough style . . . even for devils.)

We say control. And there is another so called "controversy" giggling up blood like a gagging cave-ite drenching
our Black consciousness. Hate Hate . . . hot faced and
speechless! The simple striking arm. What can the Black
Man Say? But Fuck You man! Fuck you all! But the strong
move will be when all of us say that together, like all of
us say fuck you! Then comes control. Black control.

The Callahan affair was the other "controversy." A
certain Mr. Callahan* was supposed to get a good job as
Secretary to The Board Of Education. It seems that there
was also a Negro named Parker who alot of folks thought
should've got the job. A lot of Black folks. NoNeck had
a political commitment to give Callahan the job . . . plus
an emotional one. Callahan had a high school education
. . . Parker, the spook, degrees' mama-plus 87% school
enrollment-Black-minority representation on Bd. of Ed.
&c., &c. . Verdict: Callahan. Addonizio said For all the
people I choose Callahan! And the Black people made polite protest then more fittingly impolite protest, Even some
wd be Toms shouted at NoNeck his thing was so ugly.

Rumors. Each weekend night there's talk of beatings.
If you ever been up against the cops (or even seen them
in action) in Newark you know why the rumors. Cops are
very heavy handed South type; the colored ones too like
to swing, but not in killer madness like Sinatra and

* Indicted w, Addonizio, 1970.

O'Brien's brothers who will tell you straight off they'd like to kill you (if you Black). These police are w/o sophistication and cowardly. Very frightened of Black people . . . their only impulse is to go for their piece whether traffic violation or loud party. The picture in *Life* magazine of the calm dispatch w/which the cop put a bullet in the young man's back, wounding a child, and while both lay bleeding he began to put some more shells in his pump gun.* White Cop Black Death Syndrome!

The fear again is responsible for most of the killing and beating. Their fear and their hatred. Because let no one forget that white people hate us much more than we hate them. And they started the hating business, brother. They took you from your home to make money off your ass. The hatred of the Black Man, like Rap sd about violence, is 'Merican as Lady Bird's hideousness.

The hatred and murder of the Black man is old shit in Merica. Do not forget that. None of this stuff is new, We have been beat and killed before, but we are still here and stronger that we was.

The cabdriver Smith could be a focus. But what spark is needed? Like they want Rap's ass or Stokely for inciting. But if the sparks from clicking your teeth together make flame . . . you around some combustible shit.

Did we make this concoction of Hate leaning to explode? If we are men . . . dog . . . if we are only live even yr physics sez react. ⬆.The Symbol ⬆.Explode.

You try to talk to a Newark Policeman. He says WHATTA YOU WANT? SHUT UP?? GET OUTTA HERE! These are the first words in the policeman's handbook: WHAT? WHATTA YOU A WISE GUY? Dumb bastards.

People were lined up on 17th Ave between Hayes Homes and the precinct. Core's Curvin was out there as

* A poster of this incident was used for Voter Registration in 1969–70 campaign. Addonizio screamed!

pickets marched and policemen made their cracks. Crowd
had walked there from round the Ward; trying to dig what
was happening. The day after stones and cries and bottles
and wishes bashed against the precinct. John Smith, a cab
driver, had been beaten. "Man they beat his ass . . . but
he took a couple them crackers out . . . ," the word, out,
traveling. And people showedup that night, to see. To confront the devil in one lair, the 4th precinct, where they
lay in blue scheming broke black ass for promotions.
Spina showed his "restraint," in such an "isolated" issue.
Too many eyes right there nailed to the spot. So the cops
just stared. They wdn't do nothing anyway, not with no
bunch of black people pinning them. They heart and balls
are those city issue pieces. No more, no less. Six shotsa
"soul," an Italian rock group called *Bloody Teeth and The
Slobberers.* But now everybody was trying to dig what was
happening, some to make something happen. The ways
and means. All collect to stare into Allah's sun, but not
of the same breed, their separate vision. The eyes. And
shit broke out night flying shit in the air, and the police
with their shit. A heavy violence struggled. So the cops
just stand. But get them off by themselves man and these
cats will stretch out on you . . . will stretch you out.
"Yeh, they'll kill yo ass dead."

The heat sent along the blood. Bloods sent along the
streets all that night. By morning blood and violence hung
in the air walked the air in Newark thick heavy you
thought it was mus-keetas or invisible rain. Crowd was
there in the afternoon, on the spot, where last night rocks
and tempers flew, to begin the long drama. By afternoon
the crowd made it hard for three or four cars to go up
Belmont Ave. People moved in South and Central Wards,
shopping out like it was Saturday (This was Thursday
afternoon.) Something was speeding but blocked. A
stopped motion!

By time the light began to leave the sky. Something was
wiggling loose. And rumors. Talk. On those porches peo-

ple were standing not sitting. A soft summer dancing ten-
sion. People a little stiff or moving, now the young boys
walking fast, stopping with little pinched Charlie Chan
hats. By early evening and the sirens had started and
words tripped back and forth cross town. *Yeh they breaking out windows!*

Suddenly in a half hour or so the sirens were at full up
screeching pitch. With a darkness, people were running
across Howard Street and Springfield Ave. From Howard
up had turned into circus time.

In another few minutes what was tied was raging in
the streets. At the top voice full out! A road block at one
corner. People turning corners or beginning to pull up on
porches or back in the shadowy homes. Something going
down.

Fires. At Spruce. It licked moon base dancing a shoe
store away. Shoes goin every which way. Black track cross
and wild moves. I mean. Shoes. Clothes. It was out now,
all. Except the spectre to come. But before the blood, fire
and crazy spooks raged and raged. Windows, one bunch
just wanted to tear out glass. They'd run at it and smash
it out, and keep gettin up. Then the takers wd leap
through. And all that stuff they seen on television wd come
out too. Hip lamps super trash chairs. Cameras. Scotch
was the preference my man scotch . . . the best. Wine is
madness survival and it stayed put. Except Harvey by the
case. What you see in the movies these cool white folks
got.

When the mad red eye turned on near you everybody
swept away. Crack crack. Devil waving death. Crack. Bicycles. Weird lamps. Tooth paste. All gettin' up. All the
windows in Foodtown tore out. Folks jumping through.
Them carts, sometimes, sailing full of stuff. People shopping. All kinds hip bargains. Fire sale! No sale, at all.

If you could feel that. Smoke and flame in the wind.
If you could see that, in it, the coming attractions of the
actual fall of devildom! Alhomdulillah!

The wounded Blacks . . . from falls or bullets or flying paddy wagons lay on the ground, except when some
Black people in cars moved to pick them up . . . but
still they had to go to the Devil's hospitals, and gunshot
wounded were arrested on the spot. In the hospital by
midnight lines and stacks of Black people. Women bayo-
neted, shot in the breast clothes torn off screaming
and crying in the halls. "You a poet?" a small semitic eye-
glassed nose, "Itll be along time before you write anymore
poetry." A thing like a smile slithered through the vomit
wheels and humanoid engines. This was a "doctor" speaking, in The City Hospital.

4 dead that night. 10 killed the next. As the blood, the
spectre crouched in even the shiny America, opened the
wop's noses and their state police brothers. They began
killing, when the word was given. Shotguns spitting like
the live dicks of their fantasies. They walked down the
center of the streets shooting. For every so-called sniper's
bullet, the police issued 1000 rounds. In all directions. Yet
where were the snipers?? Have any been captured?? Can
anyone prove such a thing as a Black sniper exists??
Most of the sniper stories were started by devils to legiti-
mize their murdering. But it was not snipers who were
killed, but any (black) body. Where there was the actual
danger of someone having something to shoot back at
police, &c. they hit the ground like they wanted to go
through it.

Saturday night some Brothers shot into the jail. Shot
out the round bulb lights in front of the jail. Crackers
thought it came from a factory roof cross from the jail.
Suddenly all the devil music playing on the radio (Joni
James or one of them no singin' bitches) was turned up
full blast on the radio, the lights all over the jail are
turned out. The brothers pop pop pop. Dudes hitting the
concrete floor, the pavement, and it was a full five minutes before any of the national guard and police and stuff
returned the fire. By that time they were shooting at the

night. A great swell of happy Black noise rocks the jail
and the guards shrink into the shadows quiet and breath-
ing heavy. They ease down the stairs to the center, and
huddle down there, getting their pieces checked out.

For this fear, this centuries of fear and hatred, bodies
are on roofs, to be gotten down silently at night, in vans,
to the morgue, disposed of however, the grim ugly faces
of the beasts that must do this, and want this for you,
and your children. Shooting small boys carrying garbage,
shooting someone 39 times, 5 in the top of the skull. Bayo-
neting young women, flinging women and babies against
walls. (We saw this from the jail, on the Wilsey Street
side, a car pulled slowly around Warren Street coming up
New Street, very slowly, in the direction of the jail. This
was Saturday afternoon. The Guards flopped down on
their stomachs immediately there were no words ex-
changed, in broad daylight, they began shooting raking
the car over. The brother inside, stopped and tried to back
up to pull back around the corner . . . the guard kept
shooting. Inside the car two Black couples and a child.
When the car stopped the doorpushed open, and one of
the women came out clutching her breast crumpling to
the ground blood all over the front of her. The other
woman with a child, one punk threw against the wall.
Later that same goddam night some nigger guard tries to
run the tale of a Sniper getting the woman, when half the
goddam jail was looking right down at what happened.
"We should do that to one of their goddam devil bitches.
See how they like that. Shoot one of them pale bitches
through her fuckin titty then see how these Crackers
could dig that," a brother said, shouting through the bars
at everybody.) To say what. Ask for what. From whom.
For what. Are you madness trickling out of an ear?

Why Brother Malcolm said we must seek to interna-
tionalize our situation. Why we must go to the United
Nations and charge genocide and call for intervention by
the world body. It is stupid to seek justice from the un-

just, from the murderer. As long as we are contained in the lie of a "domestic issue" we will be dealt with by these crackers in ways that they see fit. Tanks rolling up our streets to preserve white rule, white economic exploitation, to keep the money flowing out of our cities, our cities where our children cannot even spell their own names, our cities with torn down shacks full of vermin and disease, these cities that we now must take control of, in order to live. These tanks rolling, and these mad gunmen from the suburbs here to maintain white rule in yet another of their colonies. And they can sit in those shadowy suburbs and justify the roaches, and rats, the 13-story projects, the unemployment, the huge proportion of Black soldiers in Viet-Nam, Slavery, the misery of the rest of the world's peoples, then send actual murderers to maintain their diseased hold on the world.

There is no connection between us and them. Not in anyone's minds but the paid for and the cruelly misdirected. It was never about law and order in Newark. But about Force. It was never about Right in Newark, but about Power. Power legitimatizes anything . . . even fags and beasts. White people murdered Black People in Newark. They are readying to do it again. They murdered in the name of White Needs. The primal energy drive of their "lives." Just as they have been tearing down our houses and keeping our children in dumps they call schools, because of White Needs. If they did not need these things they would not exist. In those "calm" suburbs no feeling exists for human life, only the artificially inseminated beep of white destiny as it passes out to us with Dick Van Dyke and Andy Williams. Some of our children were killed to make the world safe for The Flintstones and Johnny Carson.

In the nightmare of our lives as slaves for white people, where an evil cracker named Lyndon Johnson is supposed to mean something to us, other than Enemy, and fat Italians who tell us they want to kill us or cut off our joints so they can sleep in peace, are characterized by other enemies as our Guardians and fellow countrymen, it is the part of the nightmare where the exit looms sudden large and necessary. We must get out of this definition the white man has us believing of ourselves as "Americans." We have never been anything but the chattel of so-called free men. As long as we are "Americans" we will be the chattel of free men. As long as we seek domestic solutions to our "problems" with white power we will be dealt with as the chattel of free men. In order to be free we must first be absolutely separate from this society. These cities: Newark, Gary, Washington, Detroit, Richmona, Harlem, Oakland, East St. Louis, Bedford-Stuyvesant, &c. any large concentration of Black People . . . these cities are in reality city-states, leaderless most times, almost always disunified, but these are our kingdoms, and this is where we first must rule.

This is the only way we can provide decent education for our children, decent homes for our families, a livelihood for ourselves. We are the promise of humanity here in the Western world. But we cannot live in peace or harmony or with intelligent disposition of our energies while we are slaves. Why should we be a part of a society in which we are slaves? Does it make sense? The cities must be Black ruled or they will not be ruled at all! These colonies spread around the globe are responsible for the luxury of the devils and they are spread around this country for the same reason. The only way we will keep wealth and health in our communities is to build businesses and industries of our own. The white man kills competition. We do not want to be with him. We want to be together. We want to have lives which we can enjoy, in our own Black way. We have our music. We have our art. We have our athletes. We have our religions. We have our Black science, older than any on the planet. We have our beautiful people able to do anything and make anything and bring anything into being. We are happy even while enslaved by vicious animals. *In the fact of feeling is the testing of the soul and the future evolution of men.* We will make cities, even cities like Newark, beautiful thrones of man and testaments to the ecstatic vision of the soulful. The white man is not cultured. He knows neither James Brown nor John Coltrane. In the halls of his government when John Coltrane died there was no memorial. They have never even heard of him. How can they judge us? *They do not even understand HOW we feel!*

The stories the rumors the facts of death and murder are everywhere. We know what happened, just as we have always known. We have told white people before what was happening, ie, that we were suffering, &c. From the very first fucking second of our "relationship." After 300 years my man you think there's anything hoppening?? No happenins. What will evolve is the future, as usual. The Black Man will be free. That is written in all the holy books.

In Newark, after the five days. A weak stone against the temple too briefly. Boarded up windows all up Springfield, 14th, 15th avenues. Complete wipe out of the cheap kikey biznesses of Prince and Spruce, &c. Merchants want protection. Addonizio leans against the window looking out at "his city," wondering what it is he can give us to kill us. We will make a sacrifice of his body to Shango.

Core has mounted a recall drive of Addonizio. With 25% of the registered voters signing a petition NoNeck could be put out right now way before 1970. If it works it will be the start. Somehow, as if it were Portuguese Guinea, where the brothers are digging out, setting the necessary fires, they are already building schools and homes. (Yes it is all over the planet this move to free ourselves! We Colored People Will Be Free!) This must be our way too. Together. Even while we fight. However we must fight.

Unless we Black People can come into peaceful power,

and begin the benevolent rule of the just, the next phase
of armed rebellion will burn Newark to the ground. This
time City Hall and the rest of the GrecoRoman bullshit
goes down too, including the last of these GrecoRomans
themselves. Yet even so we will inherit this city and rebuild it, once the Jews and Italians and Irish have fled.
We will rebuild and turn the city into a Black heart beat.

The elections would be beginning, but we cannot trust
elections. We must trust to the building of strong Black
forces. The Italians will have and have always, just as the
Irish before them, messed with the election machines
(and these chumps got the nerve to send people to Viet-
Nam to check out those phonyass elections!).

But we must move to take over the cities, elections or
not. Since we realize the elections will be just a reflection
of who beast is, when beast is running them. Again, we
must never be tricked into acting in tune with our slave
status as a domestic part of the U.S. We are foreigners,
aliens, sons and daughters of slaves, people taken forcibly
from other lands. Now we wish to establish our new land
just where we are, in these cities or on that southern dirt.
Nothing can stop us from doing this. By getting in the
way, the Americans will merely hasten the destruction of
their own bullshit.

1967

Raise!
Raise!

"BE YOUR SELF NOW"... words trailed off the phone. Somebody tawkin always bees tawkin to each other. We meets and stands around and dbaits.

All these things, push it past walls. And dead Ends. We always looking for new forms. We know from deep what these ol ones is. What they make. Look out the window at all that dead shit. Piled in front of our eyes day & night. Listen, somebody just got murdered. You look out the window, somebody laid out in the street.

A 300 pound woman in a red sideways wig bustles by, trying to get inside befo the blood congeal. Borrowed a life. Never once today thought about Italians. May a seen one. A cop, looking out the window thinking about big butts and a sergeant and wrestling on television. Even a

night course in social economics to raise his dead ass up
a rung in the killer called Newark Pleez.

Not thinkin about Italians the sister disappears and
not thinkin about Mayors and stuff or reports from air-
ways dusteaters old and new zionist conspiracies. Money
makin she might think about. Or money gettin . . . but
from where. Nigger cross the street got money. Boxa food
went in there. Money. Got to get some.

"Hada job down neck, this ol jew was payin me nuthin.
37 dollars a week. Hada lotta porduhrihcuns workin down
there . . . you know them folks work for nuthin . . .
then he didn't wanna gi-me no vacation time money. I had
that money comin to me. I told that ol guy I wuddin gon
stand for that. Them ol porduhrihcuns'll work for nuthin."

Be yr self. Can you remember that, all of us. Black
People. "Naw I ain got no job. Then this ol woemin at the
unemployment start runnin' her mouth and sendin letters
to the house. My husbin told me I was gon get in trouble."

All of it droops around us. Images of despair and rot-
tenness soak in around us, and we want more than that.
We want more than that. We are more than that. But
balding anglosaxons tell us what the world is . . . know-
ing(?) what it is for them.

Italians with sagging bellies tell us they are our leaders
and lead us into Rat ruled compounds patrolled by their
trigger happy lunatic offspring. They know what the world
is, and what we need. Feet up to the sun, a lil' dirt sprin-
kled on our eyes. They got jobs. They get a red white &
blue picture television with famous products for free
sometimes on the morning shows. They own basketball
teams and they can't play basketball. They own fight
racket can't even fight. (Muhammad Ali was not, contrary to 1975 television shortstories, a cracker.) They
own music bizness and you for sure done heard what goes
down in them elevators beatle wet diaper sounds for in-
vestigating blank walls where somethin spose to be writ.

We own despair. And a piece of Addodopiedoops contraption. (A nigger sd. Dressed like a preacher, standin in front of the actual god with a name like Benjamin Franklin . . . a white dude who discovered electricity) A contraption that won't work long. Nobody can sell ashes. But what about catholics and their ash Wednesday commerce. That aint even enough to sustain. The whole of Prudential a big religious ash supplier. Aha, maybe thass what them dudes in the green and them dudes in the purple (the ones whose related to the dude discovered America. Where was it? I aint sure.) Fire Fire Fire Fire Fire Fire Fire Fire Fire Fire Fire.

"Get ready," my brother Chuck Jackson sings, his own slick heads traded in for soft spiritual wool, his beautiful voice instructs us. "Get ready, Here I Come." The Impressions, "Do what your leaders tell you to" . . . all of us gonna get ready. Ready to tear down what needs to be tore down. But ready readier to build what needs to be builded. BE YOUR SELF. BLACK MAN. FOR GOD'S SAKE.

And then some cracker sits in space with a part in his skull and lectures about what we need. What we need. What we need first is for him to cut out.

April 1968
Black Newark

RAISE #3   Presidents

We have no nation.* We
are the captives of a nation. Slaves of the white nation.

Black people must become nationalists. We must become interested in having a nation. We must be interested in Black Nationhood. Then we will have a nation. Then we can elect leaders, &c. If that is what we decide on as our means of leadership succession. It is only when black people become nationalists and become passionately interested in Black Nationhood, that we will have a nation.

Black people do not have a nation now, because *we do not want one.* Some of us do, but we are not yet organized & black programmed enough to make one.

We will be black slaves of white nations until we want to be something else bad enough *to force the issue.* The

* Maulana Karenga points out: We are a cultural nation, i.e., same history, heritage & custom, but we need to be a political nation, as well, that is, rule ourselves.

white nations will never let us go free of their own accord. In fact, it is impossible for them to give us independence. We are the ones in charge of that—Black Independence. We are the *only* ones in charge of that. And it is up to us to force the issue.

We must be Black Nationalists or we are in support of white nationalists. We must be revolutionary black nationalists passionately involved in the quest for Black Power, otherwise we are supporters of White Power.

Either we will be Black Men & Black Women or we will be slaves & niggers. Either, or. Free/Slave. Black/White. There is no neutrality. Neutrality is a cop out. Neutrality is a lie. So-called neutrality is just another way of supporting what already exists—blk slavery & white domination.

We are slaves now because we do not yet want to be free badly enough to take freedom. We are slaves now, niggers & slaves, because we do not yet want to be anything else badly enough to force the issue. We are controlled by white power because we do not yet want to work hard enough or fight long enough to break white power's hold on us. We are controlled by white power because we love white power. We want to be like white power. We raise our children to say white power slogans & imitate white power ladies & gentlemen on their white power bicycles drinking their white power cokes.

Black people must become Black Nationalists if we are to be an independent self-governing people once again. We must each of us give all our time, energies, & resources toward raising our people as masters of a modern Black Nation, or we will always be chumped off & ridiculed & killed off & poisoned by these white motherfuckers!

Black people in recent weeks, like the rest of America —a joke—interested in the presidential conventions. Black people saying who they want to be president. They say I like Humphrey or I like Rockefeller. Some of our well-known so-called leaders even some of the so-called

militants (& this is why that word is such bullshit) coming out for one cracker or the other. Supporting one devil
or the other. As if there was a difference, between devils,
or even if there was some subtle variation between Satan
& Shaitan, that the election made any real difference to us.

Black People, you are in hell! You are condemned to
Hell because of your acts. You are in hell smiling at the
devils. You do not believe it? Well if this is not hell, what
are all these devils doing around here? You do not believe
they are devils? Well what are they? People? Bullshit!
You dont believe that yrself.

So instead of being nationalists, Black Nationalists, interested in power, black power, for black people to control
our own lives, to build our own cities, & re-create the
glorious civilizations of our history, you are satisfied to be
in Hell smiling at Devils, letting these devils kill yr
children & yrselves w/dope, w/bad housing, w/unemploy-
ment, w/crippling noeducation, w/immorality & perver-
sion, & with bullets.

You are sitting in front of yr tv worried about what devil
will kill you. They will all kill you. Any of them. You think
Nixon or Humphrey will not kill you as quick as Lyndon
Johnson? Do you think there is any difference between
Nixon & Humphrey or Rockefeller & McCarthy? They are
all devils & we are in hell. Smiling at devils, or frowning
at them.

White presidents make no difference to us. We're not
powerful enough to negotiate w/one. We are their sub-
jects. Not white presidents, but *black unity* is what will
make a difference for us.

Black Unity must be sought after, and enforced. We
must have such a unity or we will not exist past the devil's
bad temper. Force such unity. Dissidents, White shadows,
"leftists" & dividers, must be made to work for Black, or
be rubbed out. Black is our salvation, the love, support
and defense of it, is the love, support and defense of our
selves, our race & culture.

Devils will not help, ever. They can be used as wood can be used, but fire is not wood.

Black Nationalism, Black Unity, Black Power. In that order we can move or, Believe me, not at all.

New*) Ark
1968

♀

---

* Column appeared in issues of *Black Newark* newspaper of The Committee for Unified Newark.

An article/story about newark policemen using their real names, &c.

ominick Spina is the "Director" * of the newark police. An italian, some of his people have black blood "in them" on a humble from having been raped by black Arabs even after Rahman got turned around at Tours. (Rahman ran into some dudes in wolf skins and "long matted" beatle "hair," on their shoulders. Smelled bad too.)

We know about Hannibal popping ginnie chicks for 30 years. Thats why a lot of em so dark. And why they always think they can sing, and can be lovers, & shit. Because brothers was indiscreet with they love shit, and

* Spina was indicted in 1968 and 1969 and charges were denied. He was dismissed as Director in 1970 by Kenneth Gibson.

spread a taste a soul around without thought to the con-
sequences. Dire. Bad. Like somebody ask you how you
doin you say Im doin Bad. And this ginnie walkin around
tellin people he gonna prosecute somebody for turning on
a water hydrant in 97 degree weather, and his motherfuckin kids got airconditionin and pools and this fag
talkin about how he gonna prosecute . . . "the maxi-
mum." The motherfucker aint wrapped too tight you
askin me. Fuck him anyway.

But we was talkin about them black arabs rulin sicily for
a couple hundred years. You look at a ginnie sometime,
them dark ones, they so scared somebody gonna pull the
covers off the whole deal, "Nigger, how come you tryin
so bad to be white," except it proves that there is a certain
minimum soultaste that can be laid on a person. Less
than that, crackeristic ways, in a corny context like earth
20th century, are very liable to prevail.

But I want to describe him, Spina. The chairman
(really the director, a pinball machine for his ol haveay
handed paisanos. They'd wear his motherfuckin ass out if
he even crossed his eyes out of tune. He work for the big
ginnies, live out further in the suburbs. It's the same system. The mighty out off somewhere hiding from the real
shit. They makin shit, fall on our heads. And we wondering, and buckin our eyes, or scarey or shoutin or lying
when all the time a creepy european, a drop of blood in
em or none at all, the coldest, somewhere fuckin up yr
life. You got to stopem man thats all. No matter what you
trying to do some fag off somewhere fuckin you up.

They always, these ginnies, wants to call you by your
first name. So what can you say . . . I tried tellin them
they didnt know me but thats too rational for them dudes.
You shd just call them by some dumbass first name like
Vito, all italians name Vito anyway. "Yeh, Vito," or "Yeh
PastaFazoon" . . . they dont like that. But they need it.
Some medicine. All these suckers need some medicine.

Strong ass medicine too. To cool 'em out. Maybe make em disappear. I'm tireda they shit. For ever.

You think about some mineralconscious EyeTalian talkin about "law," when just a minute ago they was askin what spaghetti was, and Mao's people kind enough to let the chumps have a pounda two of the shit, now they gonna come on like they know something. Fuck them forever.

At this moment Aretha Franklin sings her song. It's beautiful and soft, and the day is the same. How to rage against the evils of the world when you know it is perfection that exists, actually, and you in it in exact proportion. But it is movement and change, and the song is changed. In its exact forever manifestation. This and that, actually ONE. I. Alif.

I remember the alps climbing down on them with ice on my eyes. Mad as a motherfucker, but tight and bad. Strong. Knowing I was gonna do it to em. Bad as shit. I mean you show up over the alps 14 million crackers claim you cdnt make it from jump, then yeh, down hard on they ass cuttin and shootin like on out to spaceville bad. Hard shit on em. Very very bad man. They screamd. Like this Spina will again for us, on his knees with the sword cutting clean through his empty skull.

This grey haired grey boy. While we sit in houses with each other or walk on the streets trying to make a life. Trying to figure a way out of some shit or a way into some. The shapes and surfaces of life turn us around so many times. The same way. We need to remember the same words, The old men said . . . black men ages before confusion.

We must have armies and statesmen and institutions of blackness. We must preserve our history preciously against the corrosions of oppression and enslaved mentality. I wanted to show them simply that they were beautiful against the shadow world. Against the shadow's world. The obstructor of light. That light was the primary reality or darkness. And that we were both actualities. And the fake, the imitative, the corny, was our enemy. Was the real devil. THE DEVIL. Can you dig a *devil*? Are you ready for that concept, baby? A devil. A bad thing, floating around the world. In your head even. The devil float around in yr head eatin up your peace. He want a piece of yr peace. "Hunkies" is what we used to say, on the street to each other tryin to rip off some poisonfood "kits" and shit from each other, "Hunkies," meanin gimme some that. Well that's the way it seem naturally to be.

So he's gonna prosecute somebody for takin a shower, like they own the water. It's come down to that in the world. Where beings claim they own water and will not let people clean themselves. Fat nigger cops will explain why if you want to know. Diggin everything. Having eat everything. Garbage and tophats fulla shit, at banquets of the blind and maimed. Where they celebrate their iceage ignorance drinking alcohol and sucking they nose-fingers under the napkins.

What can you speak to them about? I was hanging out the window watchin bigass in a yellow suit do the tighten up in the middle of the night. Yeh boy. That's some hot stuff. Grey grey. He'd say not even to rime. The touching soul angle we build our structures upon. Pyramids will rise again in Newark. And a black fist tearing up through the hotstreets and grey buildings unclenching only to lift the stars even further into space.

The institutions are key. They believe through institutions. Learning centuries and centuries of their mythological racially oriented culturally oriented history. For instance it's not truth or morality that the enemy relies on for his heaviness, but the fact that he has institutions purporting to represent such. Even Bloods are impressed . . . they know for instance, except the sickest of us, that the devil is neither moral nor honest, but still we are impressed by the fact that they got together and got

eureka A POLICE FORCE. It is the institutionalizing of
ideas, even inspirations, that makes the society stable.
That tends to stabilize a society. We have no institutions.
We are used for raw material . . . coal in their furnace.
And it is the fact of having a furnace that is the cause of
international submission. The furnace, the institution of
their ideas. The concretization of doing.

It is imperative that we institutionalize despite the
initial lack of "status" in the world (due to its oppressive
context) because the fact of instituting and institutionalizing will be sufficient after a time to bring status, ie
merit, to itself. If the doing signified by the institution
goes on, and the institution itself represents not the
freezing of ideas, but a means of increasing the circula-
tion of ideas.

An institution is ugly when it represents deadness. It is
just a tombstone then. A death signal. The courts of the
white world are just that, death signals. Their institutions
of higher learning, the same. Grave yard markers.

As makers of the new learning, we must learn to keep
it, so that it may expand itself and give birth, because we
provide the most positive environment, to even newer
learning. We must cultivate learning and knowledge, so
that wisdom will accrue to our nation.

It is for this reason that the talk is not about left or
right. It is about black and white. It is time for us to
rebuild our own nation. There is only suffering for us as
unwilling wards of this European's. The Black Man will
decide how to run the governments. That is sufficient.
Nothing will lead us back to Europe.

Our so-called thinkers must learn who are their real
masters, and begin to learn from them. Do not talk Marx
or Lenin or Trotsky when you speak of political thinkers.
Abdel Rahman, Nkrumah, Sékou Touré, Mao, DuBois,
Fanon, Nyerere, Garvey, Lumumba, Malcolm, Guevara,
Elijah, Abu Bekr will plot, have already plotted our way.
The Book of The Dead will tell you the politics of your

nation. This is the freeing wisdom. Ho Chi Minh is closer
to our way than Joe Stalin. Both of them know it, it is us
who are still duped. Why do you think Mao split off with
Stalin. The Russians are Europeans. Dig it! What they
talk about deals with European Society. When we are
complete masters, European societies will be in ruins.

It is blackness that is the issue. It is a certain lifestyle
that is the issue. It is the square, the angle of sorrow
versus the pyramid, the angle of success. Why do you
think we think of the square as square, like, "at best . . .
corny." Go to your religion. Go to black religion. Kawaida.
Think about Islam. Go to Yoruba founts. Think about the
supreme ego. The One. Out of whom in whom out of in
which we are rest and moved.

But we must work this out in and for ourselves, together. By getting together. Dominick Spina will not even
understand what you are talking about. His superiors,
will not understand either. Can you understand the problem completely? You see you are not the same as Dominick
Spina, at all, His covering is different because the interior
is different as well.

PART TWO/ *The Ginnie Suppose To Take The Fall*
Now Spina got indicted for protecting the gambling in
Newark. The federal grand jury indicted him for doing
such. Which he has done, and if it is in his power, will do
again. That's his connection with high sicilians, &c. He's
the large Ice Man, the collector of dough for protection.
Now he is being challenged, indeed, ginnie power is being
challenged. In every area, of its existence. And Spina, as
its symbol, and "legitimate" protector, is challenged, need
to be took off the planet, but not really, he has no teeth in
actual, except what slow folks allow him. Us being the
slowest for a time, but not really, as you all have found
out.

Early 1968

Black Art, Nationalism, Organization, Black Institutions

The art of the black man, the knowledge of the black man are his but they are not completely his unless he is conscious of them, and more, conscious of their uses.

The Role and Source of Black Art—From the life and history of the people. The environment and vibration, of the people. All the people as a body, one cell of creation, united, conscious, or disunited, ie unconscious, in love with illusion, powerless.

To be conscious, is to be united with your self. It is to be in Reality. The closer we move to Reality, the closer we move toward Unity. They are the same, one thing.

To be a black artist is to go back in time for the purpose of developing and defending what we need in the present for the future. To reach out in the now where all the events still linger and build a connection with all the power, the profoundest realization of your essence. The evolution of manifestation from essence to essence. We must feel then build, so that what is built is itself feeling manifest, and points toward even deeper feeling in the change of generation, place, situation, aspect, concept. The unity of Blackness is its reality.

We believe God is literally perfection in one sense a perfect man, also the first ancestor. We strive to be like both. And what we create must strive to reveal the existence of perfection and an understanding of beginnings.

Art without Nationalism is not Black. Nationalism is the beginning sense of who is doing the living. Who is responding. Who is listening to these words, and who created them, in this concatenation. If you do not understand this you have not taken the first step.

Nationalism is a beginning step, but we must emphasize it here because many of us have just barely begun to take that baby step. Many of us are just bullshitting, even at this late date . . . at this late date, even after Malcolm, and Dr. King, and the devil brothers, we are still bullshitting. And for those that are bullshitting we say that there are severer judges than any of us, and finally we all will be judged, by our selves, because we know our selves best, instinctively, automatically, unconsciousnessly, our bones judge their fitness to run, our souls judge their fitness for heaven or hell.

The Negro artist who is not a nationalist at this late date is a white artist, even without knowing it. He is creating death snacks, for and out of dead stuff. What he does will not matter because it is in the shadow, connected with the shadow, and will die when the shadow dies.

The Black Artist is a creator. The Creator. He must become as the creative function of the universe. At one with it. Nationalism? What is it? It is important because it is a basic creative function of the universe. If we deny it. We cannot progress or evolve. Man and his family, are one unit, and this is developed until there is a nation, a macrocosm, and then the further development. United Nations United Planets, United Solar Systems, &c. Whoever is most qualified, who ever has the value system strong enough to define and develop and defend the essence of their existence will be master of the Planets, Uniters of The Solar System. The Lord Of The Worlds (Rabi ala min). All the worlds in the evolutionary sense will one day be hooked up, hooked up in Blackness. We know that the world is hooked up in whiteness, and we cannot go for that.

Nationalism to bring health back. To bring our memory back. The nation is like a body. A man. All the parts of the body, of our black body, our black nation, lay around as dumb pieces of meat without a head. Unable to move. That's why the devil is throwing them into his pot. Stewd nigger nation, in the abstract on the hoof choice pieces, for sale. Walter Washington Wilkins toes and hands going for electric fans and fingernail files for trumped up deadbeats.

Nationalism does not yet exist except in the abstract. Except as the US Organization, the Committee for Unified Newark, or smaller.

It is growing. It is growing all over the country. But it must be hooked up through organization. It will not move thru individual effort. Individual effort defeats us. Thats the white boys' snakemedicine.

Lying niggers everywhere. The reason I aint in the program is this, or that, or some other bull shit. Die lying niggers. You fulla shit. Doctors and pimps niggers same ol same ol sayin the same jive line. Why they aint. Be somethin for once. They wanta lay around and smoke bush. Or talk bad about each other, or be doin some little laughable thing they can alibi as significant because it aint in with what the white boy is doing.

Nigger Artist you know who's got our people's minds. The White Boy got em. And I'm not even talking about the

creeps downtown still worshiping squares and abstraction
and animalism degeneracy. We have got to some minds
but most we have not reached. This is what we ought to
rise asking each day. How can we reach all the minds we
must reach. How can we stop stuttering. How can we get
the most truth told, and out and in the mind of the creator
for real . . .

Not with little jive mimeograph books for 500 people,
But to reach a whole nation of people. A WHOLE NA-
TION OF PEOPLE. We must make our move now.
Through organization. Through organized effort Through
every day organized formal effort. Through hard work
and professionalism. Through the developing of skills.
Work. Professionalism. not bullshit and lies and fake out,
and fake mysticism and faddism
and in an out ism
and sneakin downtown ism
and black on the weekend ism or some kinda other sick
belittling ism thats keeping us all locked up in the white
boys slide.

New York is getting a bad reputation for having abstract
revolutionaries. Abstract nationalists. We need organizations. Disciplined Organizations with resources capable of
giving goods and services to black people. We do not need
any other shit you sellin.

We need institutions. Black Artist. Black Educator.
Black Business Man. Black Technician. Black Professional.
Black Hustler. We need institutions and organizations first
to bring these institutions about. Ideas must be changed
into reality. Dreams must get out on the street and start
being useful to everybody else too. You kept it to yourself
long enough.

This is a sacred trust. We are not children or kids or
bullshitting intellectuals. Shadow people in somebody
else's pantry. Sneaking up and down the streets pretending to be something else. All you niggers better check
yrselfs out.

WE MUST BE IN THE REAL WORLD. WE MUST BE ACTUAL DOERS. You can lay around and tell yrself how great you are if you want to and how you thought up this and thought up that, and how you cdve did this if this hadda happened but meantime you aint doin nothin. And that finally, because everything will be seen for what it actually is, not what you gonna say it is, or make believe for your sake. The world moves by laws and the law speaks truth and truth will be all thats left, its all there is now, if you could only SEE.

Black Students all over the country are looking for teachers for their black studies programs where are you. Layin around jivin.

The art that is universal in the realest sense reflects most aspects of the universe. The white boy is ignorant that is why he is corny he is ignorant of the deepest experience of our time . . . what it is to be black.

To create for the universe reflect blackness and the universe will listen. You must begin with black to begin with the human raising his head above what exists. What exists is dead. It is slow to your eye to fall. But look up one day and it will be gone, and you must not go with it.

To create for everything is spiritart.

Black Art is the first step pointing our heaven.

To get away from what is rotten and hellish and death

Death is not reality Life is reality Unity is reality

This is the goal. Wholeness.

A speech given at Rockland Palace January 17, 1969

Meanings of Nationalism:

It is the socio-economic military-political implications. But finally the restoration of perspective and the power to make definitions. The Will, as A People. That is restored. Brought again to us, to shape us, after we, have for so long, been shaped by every other. The power and will to shape, ourselves. To move, our selves. From the involution

the involve

to the evolve = (Change to)

the revolution = change

Nationalism as forming of nation, and the idea, and will to do that. Regroup. Rebuild so to speak.

A body of experience must be built in reality, with realistic connections with the past, present, and future. An organism capable of actual growth. In the real world, not paper space, and the question marks of dull theories. But

real live stuff. Living and dying. Babies and jobs. Schools
and hospitals. Laboratories and theaters. Who will shape
them? What ideas will build them? All these, all these
things are dead images now. Unless they be shaped by
health and vision. Health and vision in America is the
Black man. The African Slave freeing himself, and his
understanding.

Think about the absurdity of having been captured in a
war, brought away from your country as a slave, to pick
some motherfuckin cotton, and then joining in with the
motherfuckin slavegetter to free all the rest of the slaves,
in this country and the rest. Even to free the slavegetter
from themselves. (Wow, thass deep.) Our theories must
be modes of real action not mouthfodder for bullshit
sessions. An epoch must be shaped. A new thing has to
be built, unconnected with taking off clothes to find god,
or better living thru chemistry or orgone beatles. Marx,
Donald Duck, Einstein, are all the same source. You *can*
learn from them. This source. But to join up with them
to liberate the world is bullshit. The cartoon hippy world
of Black leaders digging Bobby Dylan. Hip leaders is
leadership. Not frulompy half-intelligent shouting dudes
jews can still pat on the head.

Rather to deal in hatred to clean out the bill of fare so
that nothing is owed. And we begin again from the other
side of the world. (In your head. It is the revolution for
your mind we wage now. I pull your coat to tip your hat,
head, thisaway. Away from the devil.

THE DEVIL CANNOT BENEFIT YOU
EXCEPT AGAINST HIS WILL

Why does the devil fly to the moon? To bring love and
happiness?? And beachboys rolling stone freaks, zombies
grateful dead are all that, and to hookup w/them anywhere fool, like it was theater, or tapdancing will still

prove out an inferior bullshit weak product, as if you was sly and the family stone or sidney poitier. (As opposed to Miracles and Yusef Iman)

INTEGRATION WITH VIOLENCE

Dudes dig crackers so tough they'll kill you if you won't let them integrate. Which is the only change from Bayard Rustin, i.e. amount of insistence. The intent, (and them dudes was laid up, them martyrs, in the Black congress with bush and grey babes, which is just no shit the village again, no matter how hard your cover story . . . which is taking the theater really into the street to put on black jackets and hats and get shot to entertain white people!!!

But it is not hatred that nationalism is about but the development of self. To grow the small self hooked up to become the larger self, selves in tune with (a value system) the morality of perfection. We are not racists. Only a negro with a jew talking thru his mouth could make the statement about "Black racists." There is no such. (Vide especially Fanon "Racism and Culture".) Racism is one definition of an aspect of European culture. It is a description of one vector of that culture. Racism is not applicable to Black people, except as a pathology which manifests as a hatred for themselves given them by the powerful white culture. Racism is one aspect of European and Euro-American culture. It is traceable at least back through the "Teutonic Origins" theory, authored by Tacitus, which began to organize people into xenophobic racial categories of descending importance under the Greys (ie. the worshipers of the Grey witch Hecate. Grakoi, Greek, means Grey). That is, they have made the world's peoples "inferior," with theory.

If we can be said to "hate" white people it is the result of empiricism, or don't you dumb ass Panthers remember. A little pubic relations and suddenly it is the people who

charge racism who are the racists. Very cool. We hate as
of a *legitimate empirical reaction,* if you can dig that.
(We have been enslaved, lynched, burned, raped; now,
nigger, can you remember just who the racists are?) We
are not racists. We do not believe in Sly and the Family
Stone as compared to Miracles because of the weakness of
Sly, due to the pettiness of moral concerns (as to context
of culture referred to by Stones, ie. white stuff which is
weak, degenerate, as man interest, can you see?? It's
descending, away from spirit or, for that matter, political
rule. And weakness of sound, as no need for whiteys to
raise voice . . . no anger, no need there. That weakness
is the characteristic of one thing's life, as opposed to, or
contrasted with WWWOOOOOOOWWWWWWWWW-
YYYEEEEEEEAAAAAHHH, bad jim trane, ra. Lives define. You have merely to observe. We were made slaves
because *we were enslaveable.* ((See Allah.))

Our lives demanded thus. They demand another completion now. So the greyboy's life demands a certain sound.
(A certain color. A certain mode of expression. A certain
walk. A certain squareness . . . ie. the angle of sorrow.
The opposed rays as opposed to the trine, the *sharpness*
of the blood. The substance demands a difference. This
is judgment. The divine science. *The thing is itself's
judge.* The racist is the liar. He has theories why we are
inferior. WHITENESS, RACISM. We are not liars, just
because we cannot believe Karl Marx will somehow bring
SDS and P & F* greys to life with a winning tip to bloods.
Naw. We will provide the winning digit for anything that
survives on this continent.

The ascent and the descent. Hook up with either. You
have a choice, but the finale will be decided by the path.
The clearing out of descending magnetism. The creation

* Students for Democratic Society, Peace and Freedom Party—
leftist organizations.

of a Black state. (All levels. It must be the mind, first.)
Black Creation is what will free us. It is the act of Creation
which is freedom. The clear act of self determination. If
the One World concept as you all have been taught is to
work, it must be set up and animated by Black men, because we are faster now, and stronger and have the
legitimate real life need to build beautiful healthy things.
We are not saying wipe out the white people. They will
do that to themselves if it is to be done. We are saying we
must have a new world. This one is bullshit. And we must
do it ourselves. It is not to be found in European volumes
on how to, or from bakunin and leatherwhips for Black
minds or marrying jewish lawyers. It is a creation, a work
of Black art, the building of this new epic. The information of the new science.

>From the old science.
History to reveal the secret lore of the Blacks
NIGGER YOU LOST YOUR MIND

In each change of the rule, of the planet, new systems
come in and the non adaptive to the systems are under
foot. (So people who can't dig Trane are w/o essential
experience, ditto, OK) Either perished or enslaved. Lost
off in islands without a peep, living quiet. Until they turn,
come again.

Space . . . The spirit passes thru the west. Islam has
been brought to the West as prophesied.
Spirit thru matter to define and understand itself. Jinn in
all states, to dig, and be self conscious.
Science and religion must be absolutely identical
Energy is thought. Translated it is a form
It becomes form as it settles into matter, as it is captured
by matter.

The experience is why we are different. Different history
WE WERE GOING THRU DIFFERENT STATES STAGES

DIFFERENT EXPERIENCES ALL WAYS. BUT EVEN
IN AMERICA WITH THE DIFFERENT BACKGROUNDS
ONE EMERGING, ONE SLIDING, THEN CRISS CROSS
PASS ON THE WAY BACK. We evolve at different ways
parallelly. But rising to pick up new attributes for new
more fulfilled epochs. We developed new senses . . .
sensitivity. Anger, wild ecstasy, language. Hey jams later.
mammyfag hopd up, short broke down, jim we was
ripped. VALUE SYSTEM IS THE WORSHIP. Morality is
the character guidance. YOU MUST BE PREPARED TO
RULE. In Evolution, whatever is equipped rules. Can
horses and cows rule men? Why not? We are not the
most conscious. As the space rockets leave, ponder who
will rule space.

But you don't have to worry about devils following; they
will do anything we do. But we must have control of what
is the result of their continuous imitation.
An army? Where?
From within, as armies and organizations "smooth" on
the outside, whatever you called, and functioning to take
control, take power, space, institutions, corporations, silent partnering, underneath the ol ladies club, any way,
as Black, sheltered and hidden by the whole community.

Finally "integration" will win, in the term of blood form
overwhelming slowly form that exists as superficial code.
Spread across the continent, accompanying space takeovers, mind culture takeovers. We must organize invisible
all purpose skilled armies to take control. Armies of Politicians. Armies of Technicians. Armies of Scientists. Armies
of Economists. To take control. We have no vehicles to
take control now. We are not skillful enough to do it now
otherwise we would have done it. Study. Use the right
models. The right philosophy. Come from the right set of

principles. Move only with the *value system* (Vide: *Nguzo Saba* of Maulana Karenga) that permits of movement. Unity will be the only method, it is part of the Black value system because it is only with unity that we will get political power.

The white boy will be us. He will imitate down to his dying breath. But we must not be Sly or ragtime piano players imitating imitations of ourselves. We are the real warriors, and we must plan the real war. Nationalism is the equipping for a breed of new men descendants of the oldest civilizations on the planet to reorder that planet. It is a spiritual heritage. You will not even be moved by my words, as they tell you now, that this is the way to take this devil off, unless you are of this culture, and feel the deep meaning. Study the history of ancient Egypt. The move from Black to white. Reversed is the story of America. America who always (secretly) patterned her self after Egypt. Because she was so influenced by the sons and daughters of the ancient Egyptians. (See *Astrology Space Age Science* re: American Money and its symbolism. See *God Wills the Negro* . . . & more) The ancient race of Black giants come to life again.

So they will be transformed before our eyes. Our struggles, our battles, with fire and words and forms, always forms, new forms to reshape to our image. The land will change hands. And the culture picked up will become stronger. INTEGRATION CANNOT BE STOPPED AT THE ONE LEVEL BECAUSE NOW EVEN THE DEVIL WANTS IT, but beneath the mad surge to integrate (even) our "warriors" black panther style??? we will build the nation of leaders of men, through the value system of Black Nationalism. And this will produce our pure strength leaders, politicians, warriors, scientists, etc. of the near future. And the scale will be reversed, the last shall be the first. But the whole scale will be raised in just measure. The age of Aquarius. And the spirit mind will reign. Why breed your spirit away, now that you gon get a play???

1969

Negro Theater Pimps
Get Big Off Nationalism

In 1964–5 the concept of Black Art and a new Black Theater, remanifested by the grace of the ancestors and our lips, began to form the ancient words of righteousness, which turned all but the very slow around. We are all still being turned. And returned. And it is good, this year of reconstruction, as the beast and devils try to crawl back into the light of day, redefining our lives in 1930's dracula style led in by the modern day Yakub, Eldridge Cleaver, who cleaved the movement for the scent of Beverly Axlerod's pussy on his speech-gesture finger. Ahh, well, be that as it is, and all the sinister jive still going down, niggers in french hats, jerked around by some deadwords many of our fathers know as bullshit, And the corpses of Marx Lenin get raised out of the tomb again

But all that is
slight intro to the central topic here, how did Negro
theater pimps get big off nationalism. Actually the same
way Eldridge Cleaver and his misguided jeworiented revolutionaries did.

When The Black
Arts Theater jarred slick newyork and slickamerica thinking about art and reality, many of us who were admittedly
jewhypnotized and white committed cut all that jive
loose, and made our true move to Home and light. We
knew beyond our theories that we were correct, that we
meant National Liberation, the liberation of a nation in
bondage. We went up town to Harlem and opened a
theater, and blew a billion words into the firmament like
black prayers to force change. And some change came.
Some still changing. But many of the negroes so addicted
to rawpork could not cut out, now even physically. Certainly not any other way.

And although
the white boy described us as black demons from hell, &
we knew we were black angels from the ancient paradise
of our national spirit, he, the devil, had to respond past
talking bad about us. The whole bunch of young black
artists still flowering and maturing. We said, BLACK
ART, We said BLACK ART IS CHANGE IT MUST FORCE
CHANGE, IT MUST BE CHANGE . . . We found Maulana Karenga who further defined Black Art as Collective,
Functional, and Committing, and the doctrine began finally to begat concrete institutions of Blackness. But all
this time, while we grew, and as we grow even larger
now, the devil had to make his move. He cdn't be just
outdone. So he did what he always do. He got some niggers, some whiteflesh addicts, to make smokedust storms
and as Bullins says, "giggle, buckdance and break wind,"
in the name of a negro theater still committed to the same
ol same ol . . . ie, whiteness. The white flesh of dreams.
The white flesh of ideas. Like they were in black face,

these nigger robots, made homage to . . . and at this
very moment, make homage to, Europe, its life, its rule,
its degeneracy, and its death; in actuality such theater,
like white life itself, is part of that death. This is a phenomenon that happened not only in theater, but films,
publishing, music, and every thing else. Antipoverty programs, govt positions, baseball, basketball and any other
area where white boys to keep from facing black reality,
drum up a negro fantasy for nedicks like consumption
by the dead populace. Negro Ensemble Theater is chief
case in pt. They are square on the definition. Negroes
who have been blown up to prominence (actually, the
founders, and movers, &c. less than second rate talents
who because of their lack of ideology and lack of skill can
play tagalong tagalong to white art, but also continue
the dead myth of black art inferiority . . . because most
of these dudes *are* inferior, if you can dig it . . . thats
why whitey push them: because of their commitment to
white desires rather than black needs. There are many
others, individual playwrights who carry the same onus
of white alternative seeking. Since black theater is talkd
about we'll give you a negro theater instead is the way
whitey makes it which is very cool for his design, the
same with black history. You say you want black history
you get cohen edited negro history. Playwrights like Charles
Gordone, Lonnie Elder, Doug Turner Ward, Actors like,
James Earl Jones, Cleavon Little, and countless others,
plus St. Jacques' & UPTIGHT, or Poitier's, "revolutionary"
pimping in LOST MAN, &c. are some front runners in
the advanced tokens for nationalism dept. Jim Brown,
Bobby Hooks all sucking around looking black for white.
Like for instance, recently at CCNY, in a "black drama"
course, following got taught . . . yeh, Douglas Turner
Ward, Charles Gordone, Lonnie Elder, and Lenox Raphael
(a knewgrew who wrote something calld CHE in which
naked white people play "suck each other off in front of
the lights," &c. They mentioned they might be going to

see "Going to Buffalo" of Bullins, but this from a man who has written more plays than the above niggers combined. No mention of Ben Caldwell, Ron Milner, Marvin X, Jimmy Garrett, or anybody who's really trying to do it . . . just white folks' niggers. In other words, like a negro history course, they teaching secondrate white art as Black Art.

(But why to rail against the obvious as if that obviated . . . like a drench of wet garbage somebody gonna call rain, the heap of colored looking people with insides hollowed out for a gold sambo award to be placed, is throwed at ya . . . ya betta watch out.

The sickening aspect is that the marionettes are so dead-icated to whiteness that they actually believe that they are beams of light in darkness. They are still "against nationalism," tho of course it is nationalism, the force of it, that made devil raise them up as ersatz blacks (ie famous noogrews) in the second place. But it is such dead-ication that devil needs, and they are little paper heroes in the twilight zone of white opinion . . . and bloods who might shout "right on," as their solution to our imprisonment and captive consciousness, will trail in to eat out the same pail because somebody will have proved to them that 1967 was the first time the word marx was sd to a nigger. It is the exchanging of consciousness, the exchanging or misdefined intention, white for black, in the swirl of unclear yeses and no's that together seemed shaped into a lifestyle of shadowy attachments to the good ship jesus. The white committed must never get too far away to relate. To make sense to boss, whether house, yard, or field. And this is what is canonized by white, but let it not confuse black, and well meaning semiconscious bloods into really believing that slogans are programs and that "pick up the gun" shouted with a clenched fist is going to drive the devil into the sea.

Everything we do must commit us collectively to revolution ie, NATIONAL LIB-

ERATION. Theater that does not do this is bullshit, any art that does not do this, no matter on what level it speaks, lyric, scream, funky shake, is no where. Black Theater has gotta gotta gotta raise the dead, and move the living. Otherwise it is a teacup in a cracker mansion.

The Negro Theater is a state attachment like a "Give A Damn" button devil wear on his left horn, with power to the people on the other horn (in place of black power, which was too clear to admit of rawpig eating). But this shd do nothing to black theater but strengthen it and because it is forced to practice kujichagulia (self determination) make it blacker and finer. There are black arts theaters all over the country now. They shd be functioning as nerve centers and communications complexes in the black nation microcosms. They shd be coming out of the same nationalism, for national liberation. They must be influencing the whole style of thought in their community. They shd be in every bad thing's way, and provide the energy of response and commitment for the soon to be conscious city-tribe.

The black artist who does not know the thought of Maulana Karenga is probably moving too randomly (*ovyo* is the Swahili word for that). Identity Purpose and Direction is what you need and what you must provide to the black community. If you are providing them with the identity purpose and direction of the oppressor you are ignorant or sick. The Negro Theater Pimps are both.

Appears in *Jello*, published by
Third World Press, Chicago,
1970

The Fire Must Be Permitted
To Burn Full Up
Black "Aesthetic"

What does aesthetic mean? A theory in the ether. Shdn't it mean for us Feelings about reality! The degrees of in to self registration Intuit. About Reality. In to selves. Many levels of feeling comprehension. About reality.

We are our feeling. We are our feelings ourselves. Our selves are our feelings.

Not a theory in the ether. But feelings are central genuine & descriptive. Life's supremest resolution is based on wisdom and love.

How is a description of Who. So a way of feeling (or the description of the process of) is what an aesthetic wd be.

*Our selves are revealed in whatever we do. Our art shd
be our selves as self conscious, with a commitment to
revolution. Which is enlightenment. Revolution is Enlightenment.*

Guncleaners abound in white america (as opposed to
marksmen) and pencleaners, and parsers, (for writers &
thinkers) and midgets of feeling carousing gently as in-
tellects in the world. We all know whitey's thing is dead,
it's dying, for more than know it's already dead, and for
some that think it's there to be dealt with, it's just ugly or
bad, or at least inaccessible, which is a hatred no faith
knows. But we are supposedly freed by more than the act.
The new vision we produce is proof. A way out. An alternative, to the bullshit. With our rithms intact, and new
ones coming in everyday. New Images Too. More than
anything a value system is what will speak to the need of
analysis. The Critic is simply a keeper of law, in one
reading. Without a spiritual underbase, and value system
speaking thru from and out of us, black son, the shattering flame of possibility lurks to create itself, blinds already
the dumb the halt the lames (masquerading as anything).
A new value system is what the way was prepared for.
All the "Hate Whiteys" were the mortars and bombs in
the bookworld, tho the other world still holds form, its
magnetism switches brains on some brothers and they
wind up measuring with outmoded, unregistering instru-
ments what is meant, but more, what is actually happening. (Obalaji does his spacerumble-galoo with any spark,
a devils little moaning steamgrind tittyorgan, is sufficient
for the super simba to take off putting rithms where there
are none which is the entire act of new black creation, the
sun, suddenly, does, (feel the scorching) EXIST.

What do you mean by Beauty??? Ornette's last sides
are corny ALL.

What is *nice*. What do you want?? Do you believe in
God. Are you in training to dig divinity? The touch. Listen
to the horn, hold it up to your forehead. Does it echo

flashsound through. Can you dig it, thats important.

Hate White is a poem, if poems can exist at all. Its rithms are the commented on by shape form as opposed a trailer of the unmanifest. It is there with all the words. Method, finally, we know, is the determiner of what is cool. Either you will throw away all of what exists as bullshit ALL. or someway it will squeal on you and sit on your words like meat valentines from Planet 8. (Which is where the dead folks go. The Satyrs. Early Prototypes for The Debil!) Lacey drawers with eyeholes so the new devil can be invisible. Yacub was first of all a new critic, but with a very sick value system, this was so "new" it sounded like the fall of the house of usher. Angels hummed it as they fell thru the air headed towards Watts, having been 86ed by the Crown.

We do not need any hoarders of all the food the hoodlums did not eat. The stale shit in new guise, still trying to make sense for the hooligans. All of it needs to be smashed. And the value system. The Unity, Self Determination, Collective Responsibility, Collective Economics, Purpose, Creativity and Faith rays of light from actual divine intelligence is all that can be counted to be RIGHT. Purpose And Direction. Not random anywhere from Euro-America. We need blood and violence and smashed up societies. And the fall is more than noise. Hum nigger hum, do your own thing against this . . . a fm radio as big as his big haid.

What is coming is new and arises out of the FIRES. Not out of the uncommitted LITERARY intelligence, which is Slickwhite Bill the late date trying to grade somebody's papers. Do it at a party!

The system evolves and carries us all with it. Revolutionary and Black. It must be Nationalist or it is bullshit. In this time, the first rung up the ladder is nation alism. Before we can evolve we must involve. Get our selves together. And draw our new style from the energy of the whole as it is gathered to dance around the motherfucking

flame of America going up in smoke. (And not no zigzag
smoke either, THINKER.) Nationalism, and *a value system* to survive past America. There is no objective anything. Least of all poetry. It is all connected to MEANING.
Poems killing white people can not be poems to some
minds, simply because they do not think that can be
poetry. Dont bullshit. It's about, as always, value systems.
What do you think is valuable. A little ditty about layin up
wit my woman is poetic to the mind that can conceive it
such, feel it such. But the stale reaction to the outside
world where things are actual happenin ming. This is the
white boy, a geng! The bullets make too much noise for
you to pat yr foots, perhaps? We can not use no old "new
critics." *The criticism now is the absence of what shd be.*
The critics themselves will be the builders. And not of pat
sets reflecting "intellectual activity," but of the really new
which will be Black and pointing toward the necessary
reality.

Form is in the fire, in the (its) existence, of fire. Like
the sun is form the natural things. Natural rhythms.
Cushitic flutes of the mohair revelation essence raised.
Not the detail of literary nagel. A point, where in, invisibility. Behind any thing is the force, the power, that
draws the six forces to crystallize, or the three powers
beset, opposed, by three, for the magic spiral of life.

Intellectual activity as the mode of, is death, for real,
is old and white. Cop from the flame itself. Worship the
energy. Not a thing but befo dat, my man, the heavy
force befo every thing.

ON

Jr. Walker's music is superior to Ayler's or that that
Ornette's making now, simply because of the world weari-
ness, and corny self consciousness (which is white life
hangaround total—ie what you get for being wit dem).
Jr. Walker's music existed then and now, as a force
describing a purity. Ornette and Albert now describe bullshit so are bullshit. Poems are and have been and will be

written about hating white people, or knocking them off, without the little tiptoe ratnose "excellence" of the arm-chair defective. We are actual on the street type dicks, and what we see has a rhythm, maybe you just cant use, like white boys say having sucked on every part of the thing, "this shit's boring," never even having ventured into the reality of an actual relationship, a real rhythm, with, yeh, the same thing going in the same place, but the infinite spin off upvariation is the feeling and the love, not the "watch us doit upside down now." Man we are try-ing to build a nation, not be hip literary lites as Exotica 101 on DevilHead Univ.

The purpose of our writing is to create the nation. (The advanced state of creation. Create an individual ego, that is one measure . . . Create the nation and the muscle of that work is, you see?, a gigantic vision . . . the differ-ence between building a model airplane and the luft-waffe.) In this grand creation is all creation and the total light of man in heaven—himself realized—as the ex-panded vision of the angel.

We want a nation of angels. The illuminated. We are trying to create in the same wilderness, against the same resistance. The fire is hot. Let it burn more brightly. Let it light up all creation.

The intent is the guide the direction. (As Maulana Karenga has sd, all that we do as black artists must commit us collectively to revolution. "Collective and com-mitting." The purpose itself is the spirit path. Without the spirit, the "blackness" is a mask of minor interest. A stutter or a note. Light is the answer, and to understand this is to be committed, through faith, to its existence. Poetry is jingling lace without *purpose*. Light has a style. Blackness is a force. All the power must be summoned, from everywhere it exists as real power.

Its criticism will be its absence, its failure to exist. Re: SoCalled "LiteraryNegroes"/
            There is still an entrail, an inside navel

connection with the bodies of the dead. The dead white babies puked out in a slow trickle and researched and sprayed, for life, and stood up and made to curtsy, an agonizing computerized boogaloo going for straighten up and be intelligent.

We are clawing for life. The forms will run & sing & thump & make war too. We are "poets" because someone has used that word to describe us. What we are our children will have to define. We are creators and destroyers —firemakers Bomb throwers and takers of heads.

Let the fire burn higher, and the heat rage outta sight.

Can you define this mad beauty now at its crazy summit. Can you pipsqueak a form when it is more energy that is needed. More Energy! The combinations exist & will exist. The double clutching tripple stopping fipple tonguing intelligence is evolving and learning and meditating at incredible speeds.

The new poetry is structures of government & shapes of cities. The boomaloom of words will shape a vision scattered from Johnny Boy's mouth and carry all the street noise as Mass Music and Sphere Image. To Destroy & Survive & Defend & Build.

We do not worry about anything but dullness flatness and worship of texts which are rubberbanded to plain death.

The breakthru the break out the move New ness New forms Explorations Departures all with the responsibility to force and be changed all with the commitment to Black Revolution, utilizing the collective spirit of Blackness.

(I say another time, the harmonics in James Brown's voice are more "complicated," if that's what you dig, than Ornette Coleman will ever be. Altho, and here's the cold part, there was a time, when Ornette cdda gone straight out past Lama city, and the pyramids of black gold. His tune was that hip . . . once!! It was his life, and his commitment, as path, that changed it.

Revolution, will provide the fire in your loins, them hot

rithms, jim. Work is the spirit of rhythm. Carry yr book
with you. Hard work. Brutal work. (Sing sing, song in yr
back pocket. Build a house, man. Build a city. A Nation.
This is the heaviest work. A poem? One page? Ahhhh
man, consider 200,000,000 people, feed and clothe them,
in the beauty of god. That is where it's at. And yeh, man,
do it well. Incredibly Well.

Nationalism Vs PimpArt

New talk of Black Art re-emerged in America around 1964. It was the Nationalist consciousness reawakened in Black people. The sense of identity, and with that opening, a real sense of purpose and direction. The sense of who and what we were and what we had to do.

We began to understand with the most precise consciousness that we were beings of a particular race and culture, whatever our experience. And that finally if we were to be saved we must be saved totally, as a race, because the deathbattle raging around and through us was an actual death struggle between two cultures.

Warfare between that which generates and signifies life and that which is death. As a confusing adjunct to this real war minces "The rEVolUTion" within white society, to make Allen Ginsberg and/or Fulton Sheen comfortable with John Bull's grandson. And that is, will happen. (If

you dont have on red, white and blue bellbottoms you
must be neckit!)

And all of the above can get in on the vague, integrated,
plastic, homosexual "rEVolUTioN" . . . a conglomera-
tion of words, degeneracy, and fake pseudo "act." But for
Black people it was (is) critical that we begin to focus on
National Liberation, which is what we always meant when
we were conscious, National Liberation, the freeing of one
nation (culture) from the domination of another.

This was the truth we felt and found, and this is the
path we still pursue. Malcolm said (to us) "if you love
revolution, you love Black Nationalism." And this consciousness is coming into strong fruition, this legacy of,
and movement through, nationalism. Fanon added, "the
concept of nation and culture are inseparable. If you talk
about nation you talk about culture." The ways and means
of a people, how they live, and what they remember of
that life their value system. Not merely singing and dancing, or wearing dashikis, tho all life function is to some
extent part of a creative motif. Whether war or cornbread.
It is a creation of some sensibility. It issues out of some
value system. The largest sensibility we deal with now is
the National sensibility. *To free the nation is at the same
time to free the culture ie, the way of life of* . . .

The largest creation, the most exacting manifestation
of Euro-American (white) creative motif is, right now,
Viet-Nam. An Absurd White-Comedy. The Ethos (characteristic life-style) of Euro-America is death, about death,
and/or dead, or the worship of. Beckett is the prize winner
cause he tell about it so cool.

But Nationalism was the move away from this death
and degeneracy. To draw away from the dead body, and
its spirit. (As Touré says, "decolonialization is not only
to get rid of the colonizer, but his spirit as well." Black
Art was first the restoration of LIFE and the restoration
of HOPE, that all of the humans would survive the reign

of the beasts. But we learned that we could only survive by evolving a different value system from the beast value system. Whether social or aesthetic, they are exactly the same. The films of Warhol, when they are about anything are about sucking people off. (They are exact replicas of American Sensibility.) This can be high art, to people who are interested in sucking people off. But that will not liberate Black people. Campbell's soup cans will not. Some more materialism, if you can dig it, the worship of *things* . . . sacred to a nation, indicative of that nation's spirit . . . an artificial commodity.

The Art is The National Spirit. That manifestation of it. Black Art must be the Nationalist's vision given more form and feeling, as a razor to cut away what is not central to National Liberation. To show that which is. As a humanistic expression Black Art is a raiser, as a spiritual expression it is itself raised. And these are the poles, out of which we create, to raise, or as raised.

The great deluge of nakedness and homosexuality, is a "revolution" within the Euro-Am meaning world. The great dope "revolution." All these will change the mores of Euro-Am, they already have. That "revolution" will succeed. But it is not the revolution we spoke of. Though the energy unleashed by our own Black swiftness serves to power the jr. cracker's cry of "rEVolUTioN." (Witness SDS blackfist minstrel show. Or Rock.) But the Nationalist does not confuse this marxbros type changeover, from old to young white boy, not a regeneration but simply a change of generation in degeneration . . . the Nationalist does not confuse this with National Liberation. So the hand grows shakier. We "support" the white revolution of dope and nakedness because it weakens the hand that holds the chain that binds Black People. But we must not confuse the cry of young white boys to be in charge of the pseudo destruction of America (with a leisure made possible by the same colonialism) with our own necessity.

Just because the slavemaster has long hair and smokes
bush does nothing to change the fact that he is and will
be the slavemaster until we, yes, *free ourselves*.

And just as the young white boy could pick up "rEVolUTioN" and apply it to his desires, so could some Negroes
uncommitted to Nationalism, so emotionally committed
to their masters were they, be harnessed as showcase
"Black Artists" whose real function was the perpetuation
of white cultural imperialism in quaint black face, even
funnier, like rag time, in white face over black face over
Negro Skin over White Mind. That's heavy ain't it? And
where we said Black Art, Negroes with grants were set up
in Soul Food Thea-tuhs to hustle ears, and nostrils, and
plenty of I's, in place of the righteous food of the Spirit.
Skin was (is) hustled as content. The content was, like
Eddie Albee, pizen. The content, was (is) like National
Football League Quarterbacks, white.

Black Art is the change of content to the survival of a
race and culture, as itself. It is John Coltrane not Mantan
Moreland disguised as Lawrence Welk disguised as Mantan Moreland, The Elder Ward of the White State who
long ago convinced himself he was Flash Gordone.

In Black Ritual Art, it is Bullins, and Milner, and
Garrett, and Marvin X, Yusef Iman, Rob Penny, Furaha,
Katibu, Yusef Rahman, Damu, Mchochezi, and Hilary,
Barbara Teer, National Black Theater, early Boissière,
Norman Jordan, and innumerable young brothers and
sisters in Black communications satellites all over the
planet.

If the artist is the raised consciousness, and this is
what the Black Artist strives to be, the raised consciousness of a people. Precise. Specific. From the particular to
the general to the universal to the cosmic, and on back
to the single instance of love in the west market street
barber shop. (But the Black Man is an artist when he
realizes the profundity of his specific placement in the
world and seeks to render it into intelligibility to make it

meaningful by describing it with his life. There is no such thing as Art and Politics, there is only life, and its many registrations.) If the artist is the raised consciousness then all that he touches, all that impinges on his consciousness must be raised. We must be the will of the race toward evolution. We must demand the spiritual by being the spiritual. THE LARGEST WORK OF ART IS THE WORLD ITSELF. The potential is unlimited. The consciousness of men themselves must be raised. The creation of Cities. Of Institutions. Governments. Treaties. Ceremonies. Public Rituals of The Actual World. The Nation. These are the only things worthy of the true Black Artist's consciousness. The Re-creation of The Actual World. Garvey the artist. Malcolm the artist. Touré the artist. Nyerere the artist. Karenga the artist. &c. In order for the creations of the idea world to be valid they must speak as Karenga says Collectively, Functionally, and Committedly. That is Black Art must be Collective, is the spirit of the whole Nation. It must be Functional, it must have a function in the world to Black people. It must also commit Black people to the struggle for National Liberation.

But just as robot kneegrows, lustful winduptoys created by massa in response to the power of Black Nationalism, mack around the pseudo "liberated zones" of America being black, as Weldon Smith says, "for a quick fuck," in for instance literature, theater, graphics, &c. so there are these same pimps, like the dream fulfillment numbers of panting whiteladies who feared their peeholes would dry up under the sudden late SNCC, late Malcolm decamp of young Black people from out the various villages, Haight-Ashburys, &c. existing in the main area of "the movement" itself.

Frankly the Panthers, no matter the great amounts of sincere but purposefully misled brothers, getting shotup because some nigger was emotionally committed to white people, are extreme examples of PimpArt gone mad. It is a spooky world when the Negro Ensemble Theater and

The Black Panther Party (post Huey) can both suddenly
exist as large manipulative symbols of white power and
white ideology.

Around the time of Malcolm's death, a Nationalistic
spirit moved Black people. There was a sense of Umoja
(Unity) that seemed to band us all together against the
devil. But with the incarceration of Huey, and the move
by Cleaver into the chief strategist's seat, the Panthers
turned left on Nationalism, and turned left on Black people. And the love of Beverly Axelrod has left terrible Marx
on the dirty Lenin Black people have been given by some
dudes with some dead 1930's white ideology as a freedom
suit. Instead of ol' swishy Bayard Rustin now we gets violent integrationists. Wow!

So the blunt negativism and plain out whiteness of
PimpArt, which would kill us for wanting freedom. Which
will show itself on the stage. Or show itself weekend week-
out in the streets, by misguided dudes who think by saying "Pick Up The Gun," that the devil will wither up and
die, or just by picking up that literal gun, without training, using the same sick value system of the degenerate
slavemaster, the same dope, the same liquor, the same
dying hippy mentality, that they will liberate all the slave
peoples of the world. NO.

It will be a Black Ideology of Change, as perhaps an
aggregate of world information, that will free us. Lenin,
Marx and Trotsky, or O'Neil, Beckett, and the Marat-Sade
dude, are just the names of some more "great white men."
There are other dudes who will give you other lists like
Washington, Jefferson, Adams, or Paul McCartney, Cream,
Grateful Dead, or Mozart, Pinky Lee and the fag with the
health tv show. They are just lists of white people.

I can learn from anybody and anything. I could learn
something from a pile of Nixon under a stoop. But I will
not confuse my identity with its. This is the Nationalist's
position. We must survive (and this is the only way we
will survive) as a nation, as a culture. We are against the

"depersonalization of African Culture" (to quote Touré again). But we must understand that Black as Karenga says is Color (race), Culture, and Consciousness. And Black Art, and any movement for National Liberation, must be all three, if they are to be legitimate.

We know we are a Black race, we can look at ourselves, tho I guess there are still dudes who really want to be somethingother than Black . . . I think I read about some dude who thought he was an Indian, which would really be weird, like a white mind in a blood's head with an Indian mask on. Can you dig it? That Black is easy, the racial one. The second Black is the culture. Surely you know the difference between John Coltrane and Lawrence Welk. Or DaVinci and Bernini. Or myself in my green vine coming around the corner and Robert Lowell. Or between James Brown and Big Brother or Mozart's Mother. It's some difrunce man. I know you know. The attitude that is the culture. Simply, the way people live. The way they bees, feeling. The conglomerate concretization of their feelings, as religion, politics, history, social organization, economic organization, creative motif, and ethos—how they doos it.

Black as consciousness is the knowledge that we are Black by race and Black by culture, and that we must benefit Black by living, if our life is to have positive meaning. Brother JB is a good example. When he sang "America," he was still Black as color, the song was an example of Afro-American culture, an R&B song for sure, but it did not have the consciousness of Black, so it could not be called Black. To sing lies about America is not beneficial to the Black Nation, therefore it is not conscious of Blackness. It is white manipulation, like a Cocacola commercial on a soul station. Colored Form, and like PimpArt, white content.

So the neo-leftist bloods confusing the struggle, they are colored in form but with white content. Dignifying a deathmotion that had been laid to rest many of us thought,

only to see it rise Bela Lugosi style to suck some negroes'
blood.

But the rationale is always just a plastic transparent
nutout suit to cover the old commitment to whiteness. To
white ideas and to white meat. Most of these negroes who
will call nationalists racists just feel a draft because they
are sleeping white. Racism is a theory, as life motif, of
why something is inferior, check out Tacitus and "The
Teutonic Origins" theory of White first, with the rest of
life sloping off xenophobically down the scale to bad us.
We are not racists, when we accuse white people, it is
based on still observable phenomena. No theories. We did
not make up colonialism, slavery, slumdeath and murder
to justify Nationalism. We are not Nationalists because
of the devil. We would be Nationalists if there were no
devil.

New York Times, November 1969
Rhythm, 1970

7 Principles of US
Maulana Karenga & The Need
for a Black Value System

UMOJA—(Unity)—To strive for and maintain unity in the family, community, nation and race.

KUJICHAGULIA (Self-Determination)—To define ourselves, name ourselves, and speak for ourselves, instead of being defined, and spoken for by others.

UJIMA (Collective Work and Responsibility)—To build and maintain our community together and to make our brothers and sisters problems our problems and to solve them together.

UJAMAA (Cooperative Economics)—To build and main-

tain our own stores, shops and other
businesses and to profit together from
them.

NIA   (Purpose)—To make as our collective vocation the
building and developing of our com-
munity in order to restore our people
to their traditional greatness.

KUUMBA   (Creativity)—To do always as much as we
can, in the way we can in order to
leave our community more beautiful
and beneficial than when we inherited
it.

IMANI   (Faith)—To believe with all our heart in our parents, our teachers, our leaders, our
people and the righteousness and victory of our struggle.

(The 7 principles are 7 because the number is a mean-
ing-symbol for this world. As a throw of dice it speaks of
spiritual concepts and scientific principles. It is because
of this that the seventh day was the culmination, as a
period of devotion and meditation, for the 6 days of divine
work. Sun-Day. So Maulana speaks of spiritual concepts
& scientific principles embodied as a morality system—
complete in itself, as a contemporary Black philosophy old
as the sun.)

The 7 principles are the spine and total philosophy of
the US organization. They are simple in what they say,
but total in that they evoke all the levels of meaning associated with philosophical systems.

The 7 principles are "10 commandments" yet more profound to us—US because they are pre and post 10 commandments at the same time. If there is *UMOJA*, for instance thou cannot kill, steal, bear false witness, commit

adultery, or any of the things the western world thrives on. The commandments are fulfilled by the initial need of blackness for unity—oneness.

But unity is political too. The meaning vibrates as a totality. Spiritual unity is the needed completion of physical & mental unity. (The doctrine is made up of the three sides of the ancient pyramid—physical—mental and spiritual—in each of its statements. The three pyramids of the US symbol meaning "our traditional greatness," and by this, our traditional understanding.) The 7 principles are solutions to the political dilemma of Black people. I would say solutions to the political dilemma of all men, but I recognize we are different by virtue of our concerns and the context of our lives. We, the different peoples, are as different rays of light, each bent to particular articulation of the initial life force, and at different stages of evolution (self-consciousness). All men would benefit by the 7 principles. But the Black man has created them out of his *specific* need. The balancer of East and West, completer of this cycle.

Umoja (definition: To strive for and maintain unity in the family, community, nation and race) We are a *body* of people, the large Being of Blackness. The many of us are parts of the body. The whole cannot function *as it will* (Kujichagulia—Self-Determination) if it is scattered, the head one place, the heart another. Physical unity. Mental Unity. We must think one way of total movement to liberate ourselves. Each has a function but as complimentary parts of a whole. All organizations, *organs* really, they must function as of the whole body.

Ujima—Collective Work & Responsibility. All of the organs must function by the same will. We must have a head with control over all the organs. The I's must be our many eyes and be a basis for seeing in all the places.

One being in harmony with itself, this is the first need
to be satisfied before we can deal with an outside world.
But it is internal unity that makes a single will, which is
self determination. What we will be what we will do are
questions only we ourselves have the proper answers to.

The concept of *oneness* is old and Black and spiritual.
The One God. And the 7 principles are a religious creed,
in its most practical application, a code of common morality.

We need a value system to be predictable in our be-
havior, Maulana has said. Predictable, meaning stable,
pointed toward a single goal. The liberation of our soul,
mind and body. A value system is the spine of all cultures.
What is good or bad aside from specific interpretation in
specific context? But thru unity, we arrive at self-determination and can then proceed to collective work and responsibility (in the organs, or as each one teach one, or
painting a wall) *Ujima*. The value system selects the goal
we apply ourselves to it, live by it, the rest follows. Why
Moses gave the commandments for the same result, as a
best way to live. And they will *raise* us.

So that Maulana Karenga's doctrine is first a value system. It sets forth a value system, to be followed, called
Kawaida, literally ("that which is customary, or tradi-
tionally adhered to, by Black people"). A nation is only
as great as that set of values it *actually* practices . . . no
matter what it says, e.g., witness America (white and
negro). The value system is how you live, to what end.
And Kawaida is, as the doctrine teaches, "a weapon, a
shield, and a pillow of peace."

One cannot have a slave's mentality and hope to be
free, or one *can hope*, but that will not make anything
really happen. The freeing of the mind, before anything
else can happen. The people *must actually want* to be
free. Want it bad enough to be it.

A value system that is itself the way of life of a free man of high morality is what Kawaida teaches. A morality (more) is the meaning of what people do. Culture is how they live, morality is what it means. What it means as cause and effect, past what you or anyone else might *think*. What happens as a result of . . . is what morality directs. And there is a finality to this pathmaking that is part of the heaviest truth. To live better, you must live better. It is simple and complex.

Kawaida, or the doctrine of Maulana Karenga, is the measure of that "better" life. It is African, because we are African, no matter that we have been trapped in the West these few hundred years. But by the quality of what our lives *meant* we have transformed the West, even transformed the white man. The value system, especially as the Nguzo Saba begins to focus it, can give us the identity, purpose and direction to move to that better life. At each level it is a contrast to Euro-American *morality*, because first it is based on teachings that are superior to the practiced morality of Euro-American civilization. It is also a value system beneficial to Black people. And there is no reason for the practiced value system of Euro-America to be beneficial to Black people, quite the contrary, it has always been absolutely detrimental to Black people. For instance the fourth principle of the Nguzo Saba is Ujamaa, collective or cooperative economics. But Ujamaa is not, as it has been called, "African Socialism," it is Ujamaa. If anything you could say European Ujamaa, but never the reverse. The reason? Ujamaa is the traditional way of distributing wealth for the Black man. It is an economic attitude older than Europe, and certainly older than the term Socialism. Which finally is another thing, coming from the European definition, since the European definition is a state that will exist "after the decay of capitalism." Ujamaa has always been the African *attitude* to-

ward the distribution of wealth (until the decay that
made our kingdoms fall). It has never been a European
attitude, but rather a *theory*. Can you dig it?? (See Julius
Nyerere's paper *Ujamaa* in *Uhuru na Umoja*)

"The decay of capitalism" theory is also another aspect
of the European attitude of "world revolution," and do not
mistake my meaning, I am talking about the life style of
violence. Vita (violence or war) in Swahili equals *life* in
Latin. When we say "revolution" we mean the restoration
of our national sovereignty as a people, a people, at this
point, equipped to set new paths for the development of
man. We mean the freeing of ourselves for the development of man. We mean the freeing of ourselves from the
bondage of another, alien, people. We are not warring
upon our own society among ourselves. These pigs are no
kin to us. We are trying to destroy a foreign oppressor. It
is not "revolution" but *National Liberation*.

When you speak of capitalism you speak of the European mind. We do not want to be Europeans. No, not of
any persuasion. Just as the, as he calls them, "economic
radicals" of the twenties tried to stop J .A . Rogers, who
they called "a black capitalist," from doing his research
and rewriting our destroyed archives saying Rogers was
"chauvinistic" and suffered an "inferiority complex": they
say he should be studying people like "Marx, Engels, and
Lafargue and be preparing for the worker's utopia which
was just around the corner . . ." (See Introduction to
Rogers' "World's Great Men of Color, Vol. i"), *but are not
Marx, Engels and Lafargue just another list of "great"
men . . . but great white men,* or at least white men
thought great by one particular group of white men. Another group of white men might give you another list . . .
like say Washington, Jefferson, Lincoln, Kennedy, &c. But
it is, either way, still a commitment to Euro-American
values, to whiteness.

In order to free ourselves, and this may come as a shock to many "hip negroes," we are going to have to do it ourselves! For ourselves. Yes, the world will benefit, but they are not going to do it, any more than you helped free the Chinese! If you cannot have faith in Blackness, in the Black mind and the Black man to find a way out of this slavery, you are full of despair, or else emotionally committed to white people. Which is the terrible truth for many of us, even our so called "revolutionaries." They are so committed to whiteness that they must find a way to make white relevant some way. The Right will not save us so the Left will. This group of white people will not do it, but this other group of white people will. (Do not misunderstand, we will take aid from a scorpion, but we must not confuse our identity. Or try to crawl under rocks with scorpions.)

Another fallacy of many "revolutionaries" is the "right around the cornerism" that Rogers cites and Maulana Karenga always emphasizes as dangerous. There is no such thing. The work of National Liberation is hard and its resolution is to be sought but not fantasized as the result of unprepared spontaneous outbursts of emotionalism. It is work. It will only be achieved by disciplined, dedicated people, with a value system that allows them to persevere and remain healthy and rational and committed for as long as it takes no matter what happens to anybody or everybody else.

Too often so-called revolutionaries without a Black value system, like Kawaida, do exactly the same things as the oppressor-people, and as I said, they are always emotionally committed to the oppressor-people. They speak the same language, think the same things valuable, have the same "taste." In fact they are so much the same they can make alliances that are unnatural as far as the natural life styles of the new peoples are concerned. The

bush-smoking, wine drinking, homo-superhetero sexual
bellbottomed life of the hippy (a truly interracial tho
white committed phenomenon) is just a phase of death
rattle for a culture and a people. The magnetism of the
final death will compel to death all those with the jingling
matching magnets around their brains. An epoch passes
because it is played out. To imitate the played out is to
simulate, and then not to be able to stop, death.

So *Nia*, purpose. What is your purpose, for anything?
For being alive? If you are Black your purpose should be
the building of Black. The Nguzo Saba says our purpose
must be the restoring of our people to their traditional
greatness. One reason for the stress on history, if you do
not even know of your traditional greatness, then you will
not aspire to anything but dry rock white "radicalism"
(like some 1930's vampire rerisen again from the grave
to suck Black peoples' blood) as some kind of alternative
to the maggoty pork that exists. But neither are our shot,
brother. Initially our purpose is *Nation building*. To raise
Black people to "our traditional greatness." National Liberation, as Malcolm called it.

Karenga stresses cultural nation for the same reasons
that Mao continues his cultural revolution on a continuous basis in China even after his political revolution has
been realized. It is a constant process. The minds of the
people are the most important factor of any movement,
without them you can have nothing else. And we do not
have to settle for maggoty pork or renewed draculaism (a
white "radical"). We can have and be ourselves.

But you must have the cultural revolution, i.e. you
must get the mind before you move another fuhtha. There
is no revolution except as a result of the Black mind expanding, trying to take control of its own space. Our
armies are not yet formed as armies. We cannot fight a

war, an actual physical war with the forces of evil just because we are angry. We can begin to build. We must build Black institutions. In all the different aspects of culture. Political, Religious, Social, Economic, Ethical, Creative, Historical institutions, all based on a value system that is beneficial to Black people.

All these institutions will be alternatives to the Euro-American or Negro institutions that exist, but will exist in their own right as expressions of the Black sensibility, and not merely as reactions to an alien sensibility. If Mao does not control the minds of the Chinese, his political victories are lost, his military is hostile, Maoism is another name for what was. Ghana should have had a continuous cultural revolution. To maintain the consciousness of the people. So that they could not be taken off by the criminal sickness of the white led Negro mentality that reinvaded Ghana. If the chief of state of Biafra names as his country's national anthem "Finlandia," then we know where his politics are right off. The internalization of a white value system will always militate for white decisions about the way things should be. Whether it is a national anthem or an economic system.

Black creativity, *Kuumba*, is the sixth principle. Which tells us how we must devise a way out of our predicament. How we must build, with what methodology. In what emotionalism, the fire of Blackness. So that even Ujamaa is Kuumba in regard to the distribution of wealth among men. For the European, Ujamaa, like Jazz, is a saying, a pretending illusion, rather than a being. And we are not racists, when we say this, we are merely recognizing the traits of different peoples.

When we call white people evil it is based on empiricism, not theory. Do you remember how you Africans got here to the Western Hemisphere in the first place. (I mean as slaves, not as Egyptian and Moorish explorers and settlers.) The recital of the horrors Black people have suffered at the hands of the white makes us racists? Only to the white, or the *white committed*. Tacitus came up with the "Teutonic Origins" theory of why white was best and how the rest were not, on a descending xenophobic scale all the way down to us. A theory, not a fact. The lynching and oppression and enslavement of Black people by European, and the capacity for such cruelty by the European mind is fact, not theory. It is empirical, we have witnessed, and lived thru it, are still living thru it. And just because some dude wants to sleep with a white woman, let him not call those of us who do not racists. There are facts to which any honest man had better bear witness.

When we said Black Art, we meant Kuumba. The spiritual characteristic of revelation thru the creative. The artist is respected in Bantu philosophy because he could capture some of the divinity. Because it flowed through his fingers or out of his mouth, and because he would lend this divinity to the whole people to raise them in its image, building great nations reared in the image of righteousness. What is soul (like the one sun the sole solar force, in this system) our connection, our relation with the infinite. And it is feeling, like inner revelation, that is the connection, the force of the uncreated, which we constantly make reference to, bringing into creation. Yehh! we scream, bearing witness to the power of Kuumba.

But Black creativity is what will save us—not just "artists" but all of us—after all is said and done—nothing else. An antidote to birth or mind control! The Nguzo Saba itself is one of the strongest examples of Kuumba. And each idea or act that animates our lives must be measured against the Nguzo Saba in each of its components. You must ask of each new idea or dissociation that comes to mind, what does this have to do with bringing about unity for Black people, what does it contribute to Black people's self-determination—does it have anything to do with Ujima, collective work and responsibility, and so on. So, for instance, a "Black TV program" with a straight haired sister dancing a Martha Graham-Merce Cunningham-esque tribute to the ghetto(?) is not Kuumba—neither the dance nor the program.

A nation coming into being is a new creation. It must be willed into existence by itself. It is new—it is literally something other than what exists.

Imani is faith—Faith in your leaders, teachers, parents, —but first faith in *Blackness*—that it will win. Faith in Nationalism, that *we* can build *ourselves* into a conscious nation once again—that we can free ourselves from the chain of white commitment—this is all that binds us to slavery—*the fact that we are emotionally committed to it* —to being slaves.

Imani is the supra rational aspect of Nationalism, but the aspect that we cannot survive without. We must believe past 2 + 2 or 180 vs 40 that the number we want is the one we can achieve.

Simple faith, like church people say, that's what we want—hardrock emotional faith in what we doing. The same way your grandmamma used to weep and wring her hands believing in Jeez-us, that deep deep connection with the purest energy, that is what the Nationalist must have. Can you understand this? That we must believe past any bullshit "rationale" that we may or may not achieve based on 7 million subjective-objective variables. We must believe in the justness of our struggle and the certainty of our victory. *No matter how long this might take.* There is no time. Only change.

Nationalism must be the basis for our entire lives. It must be the content and initiator of anything we do. Always, as the formulator of any act must be the need to see that act contribute to the building of a Nation. That is our purpose, Nationalism our direction. Black is our identity. The totality of these as a life focus is simple faith, even before it exists as spirituality. But that is what faith is, if it is directed toward grace . . . spirituality.

We say spirituality because the spiritual is the blessing of life. It is what all life points toward. Complete consciousness and Nationalism, at this point, is the definer and director of our people toward that goal of absolute, yes, absolute consciousness.

So the 7th principle, Faith, is actually at one with the 1st—to create the whole, the one (it's what Umoja means).

There is nothing anyone can do about the fact of the Nguzo Saba. It does—they do—exist. Now it is only for the studying or aspiring Nationalist to accept these principles as the clearest statement of the badly needed new value system.

It is spiritual without being religious. That is, it moves to the higher levels of human aspiration but describes no ritual dogma. The Nguzo Saba would organize the morality of the would be Nationalist, give him a new and more relevant morality, to begin to build Blackness a new.

As long as we are committed to old ways and ideas, to paraphrase Touré, we will never move from where we are.

A value system is a describer of your life on the planet, how you lived, in what manner and for what reasons, i.e. to what purpose. If you do not consciously create a new value system, one that is quite different from the rest of crazy America's—you will be exactly what crazy America is and die the way she dies.

But we want to survive. We want life. We want to build and create. We do not want a modified version of what exists, we want the totally new—newly claimed but as the eastern, the traditional, the African, the Black—i.e. we want a whole different version of men's life on earth. We do not want what Marx wanted or what Abbie Hoffman wants. We want our whole new Black selves as absolute masters of our own space. (Can you dig it, *space,* and I repeat it for all these simple "Black" cryptohippies who believe in Malcolm solely *because he is dead—Space* is what we are fighting for. And it manifests itself as anything or everything. Institutional space, living, i.e. human space, thinking space or the actual planet-room una fahamu? Like they say, land. It is all space. CAN YOU UNDERSTAND??

But the point man is Malcolm never had a doctrine— we learned from him because he was straight and true but he made no doctrines, no real *organization*, and we must face this. This is *our* work now, today, to organize better than Malcolm did. Can you understand? Malcolm's teachings must now be analyzed, formalized, and a structure and program issued out of them.

(Elijah had a formal teaching, something close to a doctrine and Malcolm sprung from it, but made some other decisions. But he, Malcolm, made no doctrine.) But now a doctrine has been made, formalized around a Black value system, and this is what we need. How you live is how you project and how you will project. Your progeny your creations are products of your life, manifestations of your way, scenes from your path. The Nguzo Saba is the key to the new Nationalism. It is the key to the new learning. And that learning is the complete doctrine of Maulana Karenga.

The Nguzo Saba is the first, the basic, primary teaching. The rest of the doctrine, covering the completeness of modern experience is a Black ideology in toto. A path itself to Blackness and Nationhood.

The doctrine now is in the head & hands mostly of organization people, and a few key organizers and student leaders around the country. (*The Quotable Karenga* is a light sampling of some of the doctrine's content.) But soon it will be published and available to most of us. It is the central ingredient of the new Nationalist organization. It will transform Black people and by doing this, transform yes, America.

You better get ready for it.

Black Scholar, 1969

Black Woman

We are self conscious now, because we are slaves trying to break from slavery. Trying to destroy slavery in the world, and in our own minds. If we could destroy it in our minds, *our love for it,* ie if we could see it continuously as evil, as the devil collecting and using our energies to pervert the world . . . then there would be no pause, no rhetoric, only action, which is divine. Maulana has said, "Words are wonderful, but deeds are divine."

We talk about the black woman and the black man like we were separate because we have been separated, our hands reach out for each other, for the closeness, the completeness we are for each other, the expansion of consciousness that we provide for each other. We were separated by the deed and process of slavery. We internalized the process, permitting it to create an alien geography in our skulls, a wandering of spirit that had us

missing each other, and never never understanding just
what it was. After we were gone from each other. My
hand might rest on yours, and still you would be gone.
And I, of course, not there, out wandering, among the
rogues and whores of the universe.

And so this separation is the cause of our need for
self consciousness, and eventual healing. But we must
erase the separateness by providing ourselves with healthy
African identities. By embracing a value system that knows
of no separation but only of the divine complement the
black woman is for her man. For instance we do not believe in "equality" of men and women. We cannot understand what devils and the devilishly influenced mean
when they say equality for women. We could never be
equals . . . nature has not provided thus. The brother
says, "Let a woman be a wo-man . . . and let a man be
a ma-an . . ." But this means that we will complement
each other, that you, who I call my house, because there
is no house without a man and his wife, are the single
element in the universe that perfectly completes my
essence. You are essential to the development of any life
in the house because you are that house's completion.

When we say complement, completes, we mean that
we have certain functions which are more natural to us,
and you have certain graces that are yours alone.

We say that a black woman must first be able to inspire
her man, then she must be able to teach our children,
and contribute to the social development of the nation.

How do you inspire black man; by being the conscious
rising essence of Blackness. Blackness conscious of itself,
which is what we mean by *cultured*. Blackness, conscious
of itself. Blackness, Maulana has said, is Color, Culture,
and Consciousness. By race, by identity, and by action.
You inspire Black Man by being Black Woman. By being
the nation, as the house, the smallest example of how
the nation should be. So you are my "house," I live in
you, and together we have a house, and that must be the

microcosm, by example, of the entire black nation. "Our nation is our selves."

> What ever we are doing, is what the nation
> is
> doing
> or
> not doing
> is what the nation
> is
> being
> or
> not being

You inspire the man by creating with him this new world we seek. By *being* this new life that must be provided for, at all costs. By being a breath of the future as well as living manifestation of our traditional greatness. Everything we do must be toward fashioning a new way, rededicating our selves to a black value system. The house we live in, the clothes we wear, the food we eat, the words we speak, must reinforce our move for National Liberation and the new consciousness of the million year old African personality, and it is the woman who must reinforce these thrusts. She is the creator of the environment, if she is conscious. The need to expand this environment, to control our space, so that we will be able to create a complementary, beneficial environment for black people and a new world consciousness is the path of National Liberation. Inspire, to raise the spirit of, to constantly lift us to what we have to do. To inspire is to *be* the new consciousness, so that we must be defenders and developers of this new consciousness. You must be what we *need*, to survive . . . the strength, the health, the dignity, which is this *new*, millennia old, raging beauty.

To inspire, is to *be* consciousness, and this act alone is teaching. To teach the children . . . what? To teach them this new consciousness. To give them a value for black liberation, for National Liberation. To teach them to keep their spirits free of the alien value system: to shape them in the master teachings of African National-ism, the new nationalism, called Kawaida. The doctrine of Maulana Karenga.

Education is the root of development, it is also defense. When we speak of Black Power we mean, Self Respect, Self Determination, and Self Defense. To Teach the chil-dren, to educate the children, is to make our future pre-dictable, and positive. Our children are our future. Who controls your children's minds controls your life even after the death of your body. We must make sure our children are Black . . . not only by Race, and Culture, but through Consciousness. Education is the development of consciousness.

If the brothers are to fly in the face of, and confront, finally, to defeat, evil . . . our sisters, in that same strug-gle, must know the reasons we are struggling, and they must continue to teach, even if we are gone, whether our absence is temporary or permanent. It must be black con-sciousness that is given to our babies with their milk, and with the warmth of the black woman's loving body. Black consciousness, survival training, inspiration. It must be their natural heritage, and earliest environmental vibra-tion . . . provided for, and emphasized by the woman.

Our women have organized The African Free School here in Newark, named after the first public school in America. It is to project our children in our own image. From 4 to 14 they are taught Sifa Ote Mtu Weusi . . . All Praises To The Black Man. They are taught who they are and what they must grow up to do. What is provided is identity, purpose and direction. A Black Value System of which their mothers must be the earliest examples they are conscious of. *The future black nation is composed of children. Who is in control of their minds?* Each day many black people send their children to school for six hours to learn white racism. Finally at the end of this training they learn, and many submit, and become white racists themselves. It is Black Fathers who must teach Black Mothers, and Black Families, but it is Black Mothers, who are from the earliest living memory closest, therefore, of perhaps deepest value as teachers. It must be survival and liberation that you teach sister.

Inspiration, to provide us with energy to reshape the world. The teaching of the children, so that they will understand, and take up the task.

When we say Social Development, we are talking about the evolution of the living together process, the communing of the community, and how that is manifested. How do we live together . . . is it beneficial? The community itself is an intelligence, it is a living entity, shaped by and shaping its external environment. But by what internal laws do we cohere, as a people? By what organic laws of consciousness, that we actually subscribe to, actually live according to, by what real laws do we arrange ourselves in awe of, in response to.

Despite, but even so, because of, and also, in spite of, The Devil, we are organized among ourselves (even in our lack of Organization) as a people. A captive people. Captive people have an organization, not necessarily in the actual framework of the colonizer's program, but developed in some terrifying measure because of it . . . ie because we are slaves. We have relationships with each other that exist exclusively because of the devil. The arc of our consciousness expansion is sometimes confined to narrow explosive bursts, because we cannot grow in absolute openness and health to completely express the black magic of our million year experience on this planet. We are schizophrenic-manic/depressive-paranoid in our everyday world, in varying degrees, to different ends, for different reasons, depending on where we are in the devil's frame, but we have a community any way. For some it is brief memory, a blind snag of melody, perhaps jiggling their leg some funny way even tied up in NudeModSick-High "Life." Hippie Nigger, Edwardian Nigger, Twiggy Nigger (ress), AT&T Nigger, Scared Nigger, Preacher Nigger, Anti-Poverty Nigger (Excuse me TJ) . . . and so forth, along every imaginable string tied up to the devil's shriveling plant. But we have a nation, anyway. Our men are our men. Our women are our women. The smoke filled miniature cosmic toilet is America. That's why we cant always *see* each other. That's why we cant always really be in tune. But we have the racial memory of organization & nationhood and an actual living structure now, as a nation. But a nation in bondage.

We are saying that we gotta get a betta structure. Tradition and reason. Memory and fact. Our life style should be finally beautiful despite any interference. The resistance we turn into light and heat. The liberating consciousness consciously evolved. Consciously developed. Made stronger. The woman must encourage the seeds of liberation in her every act. Social Development means education, health, the home, the community—how it relates to the theme of National Liberation, how they can be drawn into it as contributors—their own consciousness evolving, what you call politicizing, nationalizing. What is a nationalist lifestyle and ethos? Sister you in your dealing with the creative (the baby comes out of your body), the submissive, so enveloping, intelligence, must re-create this world pattern by an act of will.

We are fighting a war, yes, but the most crucial part of that war now is the developing of the army's consciousness. To give them the will, hence the time, to resist & survive, and finally make change. To finally re-exist as a whole people. However that must be done. We must develop a value for re-creating the political intelligence of that nation. *Social development means to re-create the life style of a free people,* evolving it from the life style of a conquered, colonized, people. Every breath must be a bullet, every step an attack. Woman learn the priorities of nation building, and be an example of why we want a nation, in-the-first-place. But you must complement us, complete us, so we are whole. What we do, all our energy, is to be the male part of a free people. All that love and faith (imani) must be the connector the reconnector, as national purpose, or thru national purpose of black woman to black man, forever: the questions gone, the answers a living creation called nation.

The Leftists have reintroduced the white woman for the precise purpose of stunting the nation, and changing the young black would be "revolutionary" into a snarling attachment of jewish political power. Must it be our fate to be the police dogs of "revolutionary white boys," egged on by Sheena (Tarzan's spare part) the blonde jungle queen. Black women understand that there is no future for the black nation addicted to the integrated political consciousness! That is just the newest order of white rule. Another group, we shuffle to the wdbe music of. With another jargon, another reason, for layin up with the oppressor's woe-man. The separation between black man and black woman resets, all national purpose and with that, all national spirit, broken down. A nation is a whole people. The black woman must be the one half and the black man must be the other half of our life sign, our eternal re-manifestation. This has got to be easy to understand.

But as long as any *thing* separates the black man and the black woman from moving together, being together, being absolutely in tune, each doing what they supposed to, then the nation will never re-emerge. Our first step must be to reunderstand that we are simply different aspects of a single entity.

Black World, July 1970

Technology & Ethos
Vol. 2   Book of Life

Machines (as Norbert Wiener said) are an extension of their inventor-creators. That is not simple once you think. Machines, the entire technology of the West, is just that, the technology of the West.

Nothing *has to* look or function the way it does. The West man's freedom, unscientifically got at the expense of the rest of the world's people, has allowed him to xpand his mind—spread his sensibility wherever it *cd* go, & so *shaped* the world, & its powerful artifact-engines.

Political power is *also* the power to create—not only what you will—but to be freed to go where ever you can go—(mentally physically as well). Black creation—creation powered by the Black ethos brings very special results.

Think of yourself, Black creator, freed of european

restraint which first means the restraint of self determined mind development. Think what would be the
results of the unfettered blood inventor-creator *with the
resources of a nation behind him.* To imagine—to think
—to construct—to energize!!!

How do you communicate with great masses of Black
people? How do you use the earth to feed masses of people? How do you cure illness? How do you prevent illness?
What are the Black purposes of space travel?

It staggers the mind. To be free go let the mind do what
it will as constructive progress force, availed of the total
knowledge resource energy of a nation.

These white scientists on lifetime fellowships, or pon-
dering problems at Princeton's Institute For Advanced
Study.

So that a telephone is one culture's solution to the
problem of sending words through space. It is political
power that has allowed this technology to emerge, & seem
the sole direction for the result desired.

A typewriter?—why shd it only make use of the tips
of the fingers as contact points of flowing multi direc-
tional creativity. If I invented a word placing machine, an
"expression-scriber," *if you will,* then I would have a kind
of instrument into which I could step & sit or sprawl or
hang & use not only my fingers to make words express
feelings but elbows, feet, head, behind, and all the sounds
I wanted, screams, grunts, taps, itches, I'd have mag-
netically recorded, at the same time, & translated into
word—or perhaps even the final xpressed thought/feeling
wd not be merely word or sheet, but *itself*, the xpression,
three dimensional—able to be touched, or tasted or felt,
or entered, or heard or carried like a speaking singing
constantly communicating charm. *A typewriter is corny!!*

The so called fine artist realizes, those of us who have
freed ourselves, that our creations need not emulate the
white man's, but it is time the engineers, architects,
chemists, electronics craftsmen, ie film too, radio, sound,

&c., that learning western technology must not be the end
of our understanding of the particular discipline we're involved in. Most of that west shaped information is like
mud and sand when you're panning for gold!

The actual *beginnings* of our expression are post Western (just as they are certainly pre-western). It is only
necessary that we arm ourselves with complete self knowledge the whole technology (which is after all just *expression* of who ever) will change to reflect the essence of
a freed people. Freed of an oppressor, but also as Touré
has reminded we must be "free from the oppressor's
spirit," as well. It is this spirit as emotional construct that
can manifest as expression as art or technology or any
form. ·

But what is our spirit, what will it project? What machines will it produce? What will they achieve? What will
be their morality? Check the different *morality* of the
Chinese birthday celebration firecracker & the white boy's
bomb. Machines have the morality of their inventors.

See everything fresh and "without form"—then make
forms that will express us truthfully and totally and by
this certainly free us eventually.

The new technology must be spiritually oriented because it must aspire to raise man's spirituality and expand
man's consciousness. It must begin by being "humanistic"
though the white boy has yet to achieve this. Witness a
technology that kills both plants & animals, poisons the
air & degenerates or enslaves man.

The technology itself must represent human striving.
It must represent at each point the temporary perfection
of the evolutional man. And be obsolete only because
nothing is ever *perfect*, the only constant is change.

Amistad 2, 1970

The Practice of the New Nationalism

The struggle for Black political power in Newark is not limited to the ideas white people have about public political participation. We are not white people. This is not a simple dissociation; people are dying today because they do not understand this. The Black cultural revolution was created to teach this lesson more forcefully to negroes and colored people—that we are not white people. So Adolph Saxe's invention of a dour lamentation sounding "a-phone," and that projection of it did not in the end say anything about what John Coltrane could produce.

Newark is a key because it is a test of the new nationalism. A test of how "fluidized" pure nationalism can be and still prove effective at raising the race. We have no doubts that it will be effective.

All over the country nationalism in many forms is activating Black people (& white people too, in various reactions) & propelling them consciously and not into higher levels of life participation.

The most profound value system of the new national-ism is called *Kawaida,* the doctrine of Maulana Karenga. It is this value system which is the atom hot nucleus of positive political movement in Newark.

Negroes & elections are not new, they are depressingly familiar in any random recollection. But Black people galvanized & given positive motion by a Black value sys-tem, a Black ideology of change, is a new & vitally re-juvenating phenomenon.

We will not be manipulated by anything but the purest Black need. Though the new nationalist must believe in and practice, to a sometimes maddening degree of ag-gravation, operational unity, we cannot lose our values and become negroized. Our task is to nationalize our brothers, and *operational unity* is one way of getting close enough to them to do it.

But the new nationalist must be the hard nondiminish-able core that proves the limit to any collapse of Black national spirit and projection. And this is the place for battle, the actualities of negro political potential as *en-visioned by negroes.* The nationalist must begin with the people (to paraphrase Maulana Karenga's quote of Mao), and transform their desires into a fulfillment of their needs. Black politics Black nationalist politics must pro-vide the moral guideline for negro politics, otherwise all that will result is negro egos aggrandized at the expense of the ultimate development of the Black nation.

We are not interested merely in who is the mayor of Newark, but the consciousness that can be given the peo-ple as a result of a heightened political involvement.

We can mobilize the people around elections—they are, in the 20th century world, almost "natural" occurrences. But the emphasis must be changed, the approach differ-ently proposed, to excite our real consciousness.

What can be achieved in Black reality? Political power.

Cultural revolution. The transfer of Economic Institutional and Coercive Power. (These last three, as Maulana points out, are sure clear goals of the would be revolutionary party.)

The new nationalism must be the strong brew that flavors and defines the mixture of Black movement. There are many levels of involvement in and comprehension of what National Liberation entails. The people themselves are the material force that will bring it about. Ideas are relevant only in proportion to how much of this material force they can mobilize along a broad but nevertheless specific path toward national liberation. So that even if the *theories* of nationalism might say, as theories, alienate negroes, as working stratagems they must have exactly the opposite effect. There are people who could not possibly *say they are nationalists* who we get *to function as nationalists* every day. This is what operational unity *really* means.

In the mad swirl of craziness that passes as the day to day lifeclimate of America, the nationalist has as his focus of sanity a Black value system. It is this value system that he must throw into every game, with which he must color every discussion, out of which he must be coming all the time. If somebody say "election," we got a nationalist interpretation and *use* for that. If somebody say Alpha Kappa Alpha, we got a program, a *use*, for them too. Understanding the need for National Liberation should not make it necessary in and of itself to alienate Black people. The ultimate goal of the nationalist is the empowerment of Black *people*. Think about that. Unless they move, it is impossible. The nationalist must take what movement actually exists and give it identity, purpose and direction.

There is a use to the nation in the Urban League, NAACP, negro frats, welfare mothers, as well as the slick dudes athletic and social club. Think. They are organized bodies. The negro *is* organized. The ubiquitous churches,

social clubs, associations, mark us as one of the most
organized, in the sense of gathered together, people on
the continent. True these organizations do not lead the
vanguard for National Liberation, but that is the nationalist's responsibility. But it is also the nationalist's responsibility to see that the entire nation races along toward
National Liberation, or, and this is crucial, *none of us will.*

Fragmented and alienated, we are losers, whether we
are shot down in super radical headquarters or are mentally assassinated and content, in whatever superficial
characterization (whether a 3 button suit or cowboy
fringe jacket) to float around america eating shit & loving
it, for a dying.

Say that to say better a nationalist is trying to join with
the NAACP or join *behind* the NAACP to bring about real
change, where possible, than discussing theoretical nationalism in coffee shops, or smoking bush with "revolutionary" devils.

Where necessary the nationalist must work *behind the
scenes,* moving what has to be moved through the weight
of the entire community. If you are in the AØA or the Lil
Darlin ASC don't split, mobilize and nationalize. Make
these groups more relevant to Black national priorities.

In the cities, political power is a national priority. The
nationalist aims for an organized community. This is our
only survival. *You cannot organize Black people* by shouting *"Kill The Pig."* I know. You can only get the pig to
look at you very closely, and try to kill you. But more important you will alienate great amounts of the unconscious.

What is the community itself doing? We must be doing
that, but also we must be practicing a value system which
by its presence will transform negro activities into Black
moves toward National Liberation.

Involve all levels of the community in nationalist programs. Involve nationalism in possibly accomodationist
seeming programs. The *strongest content* will dominate.

The "integration" of a school *administration* can be a nationalist program. Integrationists must dig it (except the ones who are just emotionally committed to white control, these are pathological "integrationists" who are not really even integrationists but simply in favor of white domination even of themselves). Most Black people are not social integrationists they just want the same goods and services the white nation has. We must not alienate this mass of Blacks who constitute the majority of us. So that a program for "integrating" administrations of this or that are good programs for nationalists to get behind, because in so doing they can hook up with great segments of the community, usually segments that include professionals as well as the unemployed.

The nationalist vision is as Maulana Karenga says "progressive perfection." The election in Newark of a Black and Puerto Rican slate ie a mayor and 7 of 9 possible councilmen is not to us an end in itself. It is the beginning of national construction. We must develop the theory and vision of nation building even with a city of 500,000 people.

Newark, New Ark, the nationalist sees as the creation of a base, as example, upon which one aspect of the entire Black nation can be built. We will build schools or transform present curriculum to teach National Liberation. We will create agencies to teach community organizing, national & local politics, and send brothers all over the country to re-create the model. We will nationalize the city's institutions as if it were liberated territory in Zimbabwe or Angola. There are nations of less than 300,000 people.

We will build a "city-state," or make alliances throughout the area to develop regional power in the scatter of Black cities of northern New Jersey.

Control of institutions (schools, hospitals, &c) and coercive (police) mental-spiritual development & defense, is control over two major aspects of life. Economic control will be gained by reversing tax priorities so that the capitalists will pay for the cities needs, and the suburban dwellers pay tax on their city gained salaries. All the transportation and communications industries must be highly taxed and/or "nationalized." The Port of Authority and Newark Air Port are vast money makers for suburbia, they will become even vaster money makers for the city. Change municipal priorities so that they will reflect the need to raise a people & rebuild a city in an image more modern than most of dying America. More than this is unwise to go into in public.

December 1969   January 1970
Year of Reconstruction   Year of Separation

Journal of Black Poetry, 1970

Mwalimu Texts   (from Book of Life pt 2)

We are citizens of the world, earth men, striving for a new order. We are black men, Africans, and this is the way our major meaningful contributions to a new world, as to the old world, will be made, as a specific people receiving energy and spiritual direction from our past and the intelligence we draw from correct understanding of our present environment.

We are for world progress. So much so that we would begin with ourselves, in order that we are clearly in tune with the move of world spirit for birth, new vision, as constant change.

In order for the world to be "healthy," men must understand health as a clear advance over sickness, and strive with their every action to achieve health and abolish sickness. Sickness must be abolished and its magnetism, and salesmen, and advocates.

Leaders must represent the striving of peoples for health
and clarity of vision. The reason people are alive must be
made clear to them, and that reason must be philosophi-
cally "good," and psychosomatically conducive to positive
development, generation after generation. The next generation will make "progress," they must be made to understand that we are after the perfection of our species and
the evolution of men and their motives, to the furthest
reaches of life. All life joined in symbiotic understanding,
the amoeba, the molecule, the planet, the galaxy, the god,
the spirit. Our philosophy is *nature revealed.*

As Africans we must study our lives and relate them-it to
the cosmos. The drop of water. But all men must be in
charge of themselves to the extent that the philosophies
that animate them must be nature revealed, and be communal life contracts that are meant to benefit all men,
simply by the qualifying fact of their existence. Societies
are groups of men. And should benefit men merely by that
fact. All that exists in life shd be shared naturally. Leaders
shd be the most intelligent of men, tested by their communities, having been given their traditions by their
parents and earliest teachers, and the contemporary skills
by later teachers and higher Mwalimu.

As Africans we want Africans free to contribute to world
health and world vision. We have a "song" * we want to
play, it is communal and uplifting. It is filled with images
of how we need to think in the future. If we can feel this
song now, soon we will be able to rationalize it, and
abstract from these smooth images concrete examples of
how change can be positive. Life must be perfected. And
the doing of that is itself an eternal process, but each
level will point the way to even more dazzling possibilities.
Utopia is an African's fuel, it is in motion, and combustible. It drives us to higher equations of purpose.

* Manifested historical energy.

It is a brute idea that entangles and enslaves us. The visible invisible matrix of societies of dead skin. It will peel or fester rot or drop off. It will be bitten away or burned. Perhaps it will be a pocketbook or umbrella for another epoch-galaxy-species, whatever. But it cannot survive. Can a fetus survive? Nothing can survive. But the ideas that are us must be eternally pointing toward perfection, as perfectible structures, always giving way to higher ones. From tadpole to frog to dinosaur to Marcus Garvey. We must hold out such possibility of evolution even for George Wallace's cutbuddies and relatives. It is simply that we cannot be eaten by tadpoles or frogs, or stoppd from singing by species not yet evolved to speech. So we are willing to make plans with those who press for an evolved race of earth people. We are for this and against anything against this. Africans, now, are the unleashed energy that will force change and new vision. The emerging babe whose life redefines the world. Let all the inhabitants of the world tune in to the redefinition. We mean only good faith and good works and beauty to the world. We are ultimately constructive forces. We are positive spirits. We are teachers Mwalimu and students Mwanafunzi of nature (revealed). And this is our philosophy and religion. Our ideology is "give power to the bringers of positive change."

We live in a world now, where the real work cannot be spoken of clearly. We believe our children will get to the real work. We will make the real work possible. Before the real work can be done, the disease, the power of evil, must be cleared away. The bringers of positive change must have places prepared for them to work. They must be delivered schools and temples and factories and laboratories and studies in which to function. They must be delivered cities in which to move freely among the most sympathetic of environments so that they can study, and meditate, and create, and formalize the new learning and concretize the new vision. They must actually be allowed

to build, and to stretch out past whatever exists and startle
even themselves with the powerful beauty of human life
raised. Once *all* the people are housed and fed and clothed
and given minimal educations so that they understand
who and what they are and where they are and what time
it is, and what can be done in a sympathetic world. Then
it will be time to really learn and really create, and this is
the real work.

Once all the monstrosities can be laid low, the physical
mental and spiritual monstrosities that inhabit all space
can be cast out of our path. The substances that are
the elements of evil functioning reduced, or gotten
around, or destroyed, for the age of its accomplishment
(tho even such "destruction" perhaps sets up higher evil
on ethereal planes we can only speculate about. It is the
grosser world the grosser evil the grosser accomplishment,
before the finer accomplishment and with that the more
subtle, the finest yet still finer core tho it can also be
surmounted yet into the future by those of us who are
created to do this) then the leaders will go up and the
people follow, and at that level, the people will go up,
eventually, drawn, magnetized by the strengths and love
of the age, which be the next generation of true leaders &
angels. We understand that we are in many ways brutes
ourselves. Teeth knocked out heads split, full of anger
and venom, and murderous tendencies. Barely skimming
above the degeneracy of the swirling american beast
world. But we pull the reins of a nation, a whole people,
and were it not for this humbling weight, we wd sail
meaninglessly into the firmament, too swiftly to sample
the enlightening enriching scum of lower spirit higher
humanistic feeling-(ideation).

The earth structures are spiritual patterns fleshd. Ideologi-
cal vibration manifested in physical-intellectual world.
Systems, structures, also are ideas fleshed. Our ideas we

must drive onto higher planes and the physical world will follow. Sometimes it will take wars, always struggle, and cunning, and devotion and commitment, and plain out love. But this is the actual meaning of life. Its spin is meaningful, its gamelike quality. This is what "good" means, that which is positive, that lifts and raises, that develops. Not envelopes in dirt alone to stay there "dead," and deservingly so.

May 21, 1970